D0891393

CHERRY AMES, STUDENT NURSE

The Cherry Ames Stories

A Publication of Palm Publishing, LLC

Acknowledgements

Palm Healthcare Foundation, Inc. extends deep appreciation to Harriet
Schulman Forman, who inspired this project. We are also grateful to our
community's Chief Nursing Officers Mary Bishop, Joan Blacharski,
Carole Di Florio, Terri Guzman, Sharon Hayes, Cynthia Dent-Kennedy,
Brenda Logan, Angela Ninestine, Dee McCarthy, Marty O'Neill,
Ruth Schwarzkopf, Carmen Shell, Silvia Stradi, Litha Varone,
Ernestine Ziacik, and to Dean Anne Boykin
and Rose O'Kelly Sherman at the Christine E. Lynn College of Nursing at
Florida Atlantic University whose support and partnership have been
instrumental in advancing the work of the foundation on behalf of the
nursing profession.

A special thank you to Robert Wells, brother of Helen Wells author,
without whom none of this would have been possible.

Proceeds from the Cherry Ames Series will be directed
to nursing scholarships in Palm Beach County.

Nursing Spectrum - Professional Sponsor

Art Direction & Design by Scott Grimando
www.grimstudios.com

The patients halted their exclamations when Cherry
wheeled Winky in to see the tree.

Cherry Ames, Student Nurse

CHERRY AMES
STUDENT NURSE

By

HELEN WELLS

PALM
PUBLISHING·LLC

PALM

PUBLISHING·LLC

Palm Publishing LLC
A subsidiary of Palm Healthcare
Foundation, Inc.
1016 North Dixie Highway
West Palm Beach, FL 33401

Copyright © 1943 by
Grosset & Dunlap, Inc.

ISBN 0-9753548-0-9

2 3 4 5 6 7   08 07 06 05 04

Printed by Rose Printing Company
Tallahassee, FL

Contents

v

CHERRY AMES, STUDENT NURSE

CHAPTER I

Cherry Starts Out

CHERRY SAT CROSS-LEGGED ON HER SUITCASE AND
tugged. There! The two stubborn locks finally clicked
shut. This would make her new uniforms look like ac-
cordions and she mourned for the new blue dance dress.
But at least they were *in*. Cherry puffed and with a toss
of her head sent the dark brown curls off her glowing
cheeks. Then she sat bolt upright on the suitcase and
gasped.

"How do I look?" said Midge from the doorway.
Billowing over her small figure was Cherry's gray probationer's uniform and crackling white apron, miles too
big for her. From around the collar, her freckled face
peered out, grinning impishly.

"Midge Fortune!" Cherry exploded. "You thirteen-
year-old hazard! Unhand that uniform right away! Do
you want to make me miss my train?" She darted after

3

Midge and wormed her out of the dress. "And now I'll have to battle with that suitcase again!" she groaned. She gave the squirming Midge a little shake. "Honestly, if you weren't Dr. Joe's daughter, I'd cut you up for stew and feed you to my worst enemy!"

"You haven't got a worst enemy," Midge pointed out calmly. She folded the garments with care and bravely attacked the suitcase. "And besides," Midge went on, with a fine disregard for any connection, "your new red suit is the best-looking thing in Hilton." She looked at Cherry admiringly.

And Cherry was well worth admiring. She was slender and healthy and well-built; she moved with a proud erect posture that made her seem beautifully tall and slim. Her eyes and her short curly hair were very dark, almost black—the clear-cut black that glistens. Groomed to crisp perfection, Cherry was as vivid as a poster in her red wool sports suit. And her face fairly sparkled with warmth and humor.

She pulled the little matching hat over her curls, just as Midge banged the suitcase closed. They both hastily sat down on the lid while they pressed the locks shut.

"What's left out," Cherry said grimly, "doesn't go traveling." But she knew she had not forgotten anything. Cherry might not always be prompt but she *was* neat and she did get things done. "My lone virtue," she thought, "neatness."

"Aren't you women ready yet?" It was Cherry's twin brother, Charles, racing up the stairs and into Cherry's room. Strangers found it hard to believe that Charlie was Cherry's twin, for he was as fair as she was dark. He was a tall athletic boy with ruffled light hair and alert blue eyes. Charlie was entering the State Engineering College this fall. He flashed Cherry an understanding grin and picked up her bulging bag.

"Well, it's a good thing I'm strong and healthy! What do you have in this thing?" he asked. "Half a dozen of your future patients?"

Midge rushed to Cherry's defense. "She'll be the best nurse that ever——"

"Of course she will," Charlie interrupted, his blue eyes amused. "In fact, Fortune, Nurse Ames will be even better than that."

Cherry laughed at being called Nurse—she had no right to that title yet—but a little thrill shivered down her back just the same

Charlie pretended to bend his broad shoulders under the weight of the suitcase. "They'd never let you on a plane with a ton like this."

"I knew you'd find a plane in here somewhere!" Cherry laughed. "Why don't you learn to be a pilot and get it over with?"

"That may not be a bad idea," Charlie replied. "Well, come along, Fortune. Train time is no time to sit down and discuss our careers." He swept Midge and the suitcase before him down the staircase. Midge wailed back over her shoulder:

"I wish you weren't going away!"

Cherry looked around her familiar room. "I almost wish it myself," she thought. At the window, crisp white ruffled curtains were gracefully looped back with red ribbon. Her little dressing table wore white dotted swiss skirts and saucy red bows. The oval hooked rug was one her great-grandmother had made. Her bookshelf held the books she had carried to school and now was leaving behind. She wondered what her new room at the Nursing School would be like.

Cherry swallowed hard. She did not feel eighteen and through with high school and almost a student nurse. For all her dreams and hopes, she still was not entirely sure nursing was for her. All the tales she had ever heard flashed through her mind—you see so much suffering, you scrub floors, you might give the patient the wrong medicine, and all the other nightmares. Probably nonsense, the whole lot of them. Cherry wanted a profession of her own. More than that, she wanted to do vital work, work that the world urgently needs. She honest-to-goodness cared about people and she wanted to help them on a grand and practical scale. But did she have all that it takes to be a nurse? Could her dreams survive three stern years of training? Well, she would learn the answer very soon.

Cherry walked lightly to the window where the very top of the lilac bush brushed against the screen. It was the first of September and late summer flowers bloomed in the yard—asters, marigolds, vibrantly blue delphinium, and her mother's favorite though struggling dahlias. "I won't be here this fall to see how the dahlias make out," she thought. She looked down the tree-shaded street where she had so many friends. A giggle leaked out as she remembered the Hallowe'en their crowd had rung all the doorbells for streets around and solemnly handed their neighbors pumpkin faces. The good-humored neighbors had responded by giving them appies to bob, corn to pop, and Mrs. Pritchard had provided a feast of homemade pumpkin pie and cider. It was a good thing the neighbors had a sense of humor. And she remembered that never-to-be-forgotten outdoor party she and Charlie had given two summers ago, with lighted paper lanterns strung across the shadowy lawn and forty of them playing "Hide the Moon, Sheep" and that bottomless freezer of her mother's peach ice cream for an inspired home base. Well, good-by to all that!

Cherry sighed and resolutely started for the hall. She took one last peek into Charlie's room, plastered with models and photographs and blueprints of airplanes. She looked into her parents' large serene room with the blinds drawn green and cool against the sun and sparrows chirping on the window sill.

"You can't be homesick already," Cherry told her self with a grin, and went down the curving staircase. "Sick rooms won't be as attractive as these but a lot more exciting things go on in them!"

"Cherry!" her mother called from the porch. "Only five minutes more, if you want to stop at Dr. Joe's!"

Cherry answered vaguely and stole another minute to say good-by to the house. She wandered through the pleasant mahogany-and-blue living room, through the sunny dining room with its bay window banked with waxy green plants, her mother's tiny sewing room, and the gleaming white kitchen. On the shady back porch, she took one last deep spicy whiff of homemade corn relish and sun-preserved strawberries, stored in the cool cellar. Now she was ready to go.

Her mother rose from the porch swing as Cherry came out. She was a youthful, sweet-faced woman, with the most understanding eyes in the world, Cherry thought. Cherry put her arm around her.

"Glad you're going?" her mother asked.

Cherry nodded. Her eyes shone like black stars but she did not trust herself to speak.

"Honey, there's one thing I want to say before you go," her mother said. "If you—if you find you don't like nursing or if it's too hard for you, you won't be too proud to come home?"

Cherry tossed back her curls and laughed. "No one's going to make me say die! And I have a dreadful sus-

CHERRY STARTS OUT 9

picion that I'm going to love it! But seriously," she said gravely, "unless I'm good at it, I'd have no right to stick it out."

Mrs. Ames smiled. "Well, Dad and I feel you've chosen just about the finest profession there is. And just about the most necessary one in wartime. We're mighty proud about it. And we are both sure that you'll do good work and win your cap."

"I certainly hope I win my cap," Cherry responded. "Because if I should not——"

An impatient whir from the car sent them running across the front lawn.

"Dr. Joe?" Charlie asked.

Cherry nodded. Dr. Joseph Fortune had ushered her and her brother into the world, and Cherry had always loved him. And then, during her high school years, when she was growing up, two things had happened. Molly Fortune—that laughing, competent, tireless woman—had died, leaving Dr. Joe alone to battle with a doctor's poverty, an unmanageable daughter, and a dwindling practice. Hilton said Dr. Joe was either a genius or a fool. For why would the town's best doctor neglect a thriving practice to fiddle around in his little homemade laboratory with some experiments? But as Cherry grew up, she—and only she—really understood what he was doing. Those long weeks and months when his house went undusted unless Cherry herself straightened it up, when Midge's high jinks led the

Ames to take her delighted prisoner in their home, when Dr. Joe forgot to eat unless Cherry forcibly fed him, he was leading a lonely crusade.

Singlehanded, with quiet courage, with endless patience, Dr. Joe was finding new ways to help and save human lives. After the night Dr. Joe explained to her what his precious drug was, Cherry for the first time took a deep interest in her biology and chemistry courses at school. And to her amazement, she was good at them, once she really tried. And after the long golden Sunday when Dr. Joe performed the miracle of the drug on Tookie the cat, Cherry knew she, too, must play some role in the world of miracles and life.

They pulled up now before the Fortunes' white frame cottage. Cherry alone went up the overgrown path and past the door that needed paint so badly. "Some day this shabby little house may be a shrine," she thought. She hurried through the living room, all topsy-turvy as usual, but dusted in Midge's own fashion. Cherry automatically straightened the curtains as she passed by. She did not call out to Dr. Joe—he would be too absorbed to hear anything less than a four-alarm fire.

Cherry stood poised in the doorway affectionately looking at him. Dr. Joe was delicately preparing a slide. His sensitive face was deeply seamed but somehow it was a beautiful face, with a child's wondering eyes. His shock of thick gray hair and slight figure were like a boy's.

"Dr. Joe," Cherry said softly.

He looked up and smiled and set down the slide on the microscope's shelf. "Is today the day?"

Cherry nodded and came to sit down on the tall stool beside him. He scanned her face with penetrating eyes.

"I suppose I ought to say certain things to you—about working hard and intelligently—especially since I feel responsible for your going," he said in his deep halting voice. He smiled his reticent smile. "But I think you know all those things, Cherry."

"I hope so," Cherry said. Suddenly she felt more sure of herself. "Yes, I do know them."

Dr. Joe patted her hand and beamed at her in silence. They never had to talk very much in order to understand each other perfectly.

"How's it going?" Cherry asked.

Dr. Joe drew a tray of test tubes toward him. "The experimental part is going along beautifully. But I don't know how well it would stand up in a real laboratory. Your hospital has a magnificently equipped laboratory." His tired eyes shone. "And of course all this should be tested on patients—if anyone would ever give me the chance and believe in what I'm doing."

"I believe in it." She wished with all her heart that she could help him.

"I know you do, Cherry. But until it is tested, it cannot be accepted and—and vice versa." He tried to grin but it was a shaky grin. Dr. Fortune rose and paced slowly around the cluttered laboratory. "Once I prove this drug, I want to return to my practice. After all, this drug research is for my patients. And for the patients of other doctors! This drug could save so many lives!"

He held up the precious test tube. They both looked at it with respect and hope, for this was Dr. Joe's dream trembling on the brink of fulfillment.

Cherry felt very young and inadequate. "Do you think that—that I could ever save anybody's life? *Me?*" She looked at Dr. Joe humbly. "You, Dr. Joe, you know so much—and I guess your enthusiasm's catching—" she grinned, "but I've got to start learning—from scratch—maybe I'll never——"

"Child, you *will* learn! And some day you will be able to say to yourself, 'This man or that woman is alive and well because of me.' Cherry, child, just you wait until that woman who was past caring whether she lived or died gets well enough to ask for her mirror—and the little boy who lay listlessly in his bed for weeks demands seconds on roast beef—because you worked and cared for them!"

Cherry's cheeks flamed and her dark eyes sparkled. She jammed her hands into the pockets of her red sports suit, and hoped Dr. Joe was right about her.

A door slammed and Midge bounced into the laboratory with her hair on end. Cherry thought she looked like one of those imps who never walk sedately like ordinary people but land in places unexpectedly by flying or leaping.

"Oh, my heavens," Midge panted, tugging at her father's white coat. "I forgot to get you your lunch! I just remembered because my own stomach is speaking up. Come on, I'll——"

Dr. Joe gently wriggled out of Midge's grasp and carefully held the test tube high. "Oh, I'll find myself a sandwich later," he murmured absently. Cherry shook her head warningly at Midge, knowing perfectly well that he would not.

But Dr. Joe was thinking aloud. "You see, Cherry, the important thing is this." Midge shifted from one foot to the other but Cherry listened closely. "It can be used as a very special and marvelous anaesthetic. Remember I described cases, difficult operations, where the patient must remain conscious in order to cooperate with the doctor? Well, this drug will anaesthetize—deaden, that is—only the portion to be operated on. And it can be used to relieve pain so that a patient gets normal sleep. Far better than morphine. It's a marvelous thing."

Cherry said slowly, "Then—then especially in war, in the hospitals right behind the lines, even on the battlefields, your discovery would be——"

A sudden din, compounded of Mrs. Ames's treble and Charlie's male hoarseness and insistent pressure on the automobile horn, sent Cherry leaping off the laboratory stool.

Dr. Joe had not even heard it. He was pursuing Cherry's thought. "War . . . We are fighting another war, we in medicine—the long, slow war on needless suffering and needless death. And when a new drug like this comes along, it could be a victory, if it were accepted."

Midge tugged at his arm. "That train's in a hurry and so is Cherry!"

Cherry laughed and hugged Midge. To Dr. Joe she said gaily, "I feel like I'm off to the wars myself!"

Dr. Fortune followed her through the living room. "A nurse is a soldier," he said. He looked frail and lonely in the doorway as Cherry waved to him from the car.

Cherry's father was already waiting for them on the platform. As they piled out of the car, Cherry thought affectionately that she would recognize his tall business-like figure on any railroad station platform in the world. He came up to them with a proud smile for Cherry.

"Thought you were so busy with your real estate you wouldn't have time for me!" she teased him.

"On the contrary. I'm grateful that a big career woman has time for me." Mr. Ames laughed and said hello to all of them. And from the way they all—her competent father, her mother, her keen-eyed brother, right down to excited Midge—beamed and beamed at her, Cherry knew they believed in her and the work she was going to do. It gave her a good, warm feeling to know that.

The conductor was already shouting "All aboard!" from the train steps. Cherry barely had time to hug everybody all around and her mother once again. "Good luck!" they cried after her. "Be sure to write!" To her surprise there was a lump in her throat and things looked strangely blurred. Charlie heaved her bags aboard and clung to the bottom step.

"Jump off, you idiot, or you'll be hurt!" Cherry shrieked as the train started.

"Forgot to—give you—this!" Charlie shouted back over a blast of the whistle. He wormed a flat box out of his pocket, shoved it into her outstretched hand and cried, "Don't kill 'em off!" Then he was gone.

Cherry realized she was strictly on her own now. She clutched the box warmly and a little desperately as she made her way to the dusty green velvet seat where the conductor had stowed her luggage.

Cherry waited until the town disappeared, and only when the train hurtled past Johnson's stately red barn, did she open Charlie's gift. Her eyes widened as she lifted the lid of the box. A nurse's watch! But a beauty —with a second hand for taking pulse and respiration and a professional-looking leather strap. For a moment she felt guilty, until she remembered these watches were not expensive after all. She fastened it on her wrist and felt practically a junior Florence Nightingale already. Charlie teased the daylights out of her twelve months a year but a brother was a pretty nice thing to have, after all.

The train flew forward, carrying her right smack into her future. Cherry snuggled into the seat and remembered all the steps that had led her to this big moment. She certainly had investigated thoroughly before she had decided on the Spencer School. She had written to the Nursing Information Bureau in New York and then to the State Board of Nurse Examiners in her home state. "And it was worth all the trouble, too," she thought soberly. "I don't want to go into a second-rate school and come out a second-rate nurse. A girl can't be too careful."

She thought happily of Spencer School. The catalogue—she knew it by heart—checked with the requirements of a really good nursing school. Spencer had everything: recognized staff doctors, a sufficient number of staff R.N.'s, complete laboratories and hospital equipment and libraries, and a course of training that did not leave cut any branch of nursing. "My school," Cherry thought proudly. Then she giggled to herself. "*My* school—and I'm not even in it. And unless I can meet its standards, I may be very much out of it!"

She frowned, feeling delighted and scared all at once. It was up to her, from here on. Dr. Joe had inspired her to become a nurse but between inspiration and accomplishment, she faced a great deal of work. It would not be easy. But she decided not to think of such troubling things. At least, not yet.

Instead, Cherry imagined before her the great hospital with its many buildings and green lawns. She seemed to smell the sweet heavy odor of ether, and hear the clanging ambulance bell. She could almost see the brisk white figures hurrying along the wards. And she tried to imagine herself one of that army in white.

CHAPTER II

New Faces

"WELL, I'VE GOTTEN AS FAR AS THIS, ANYHOW!"

Cherry stood blinking in the hospital's vast shadowy rotunda. She had been daydreaming so busily that she had almost missed her station. It was the friendly conductor who had saved her from landing in the next town. Then she had promptly lost her way in the roaring city streets. This time a taxi driver saved her. The cab had whirled through streets of tall buildings, with Cherry practically hanging out the window. Then suddenly a great cluster of white buildings rose into view, on the top of a hill. It was the hospital, a city in itself, a modern fortress—and it came closer and closer. Cherry's heart had skipped a beat when the cab actually entered the avenues of those interrelated white buildings and spacious green lawns, and finally stopped before Spencer Hall.

Cherry clutched her suitcase and gazed around the deserted rotunda.

Someone behind her coughed. A masculine voice said, "Can I direct you? You're a new probationer, aren't you?"

Cherry turned around to face a tall, pleasant young man in an interne's white suit. He was even-featured, brown-haired and brown-eyed, and he owned the gayest smile she had ever seen.

"Why, yes, I am a probationer. My name is Cherry Ames. But how did you know?"

The young man laughed. "That probationer's scared and awed look. I'm James Clayton," he added. He went on sympathetically, "I don't blame you for being impressed with the hospital. It's a wonderful place and there's wonderful work being done here."

Cherry looked at the young doctor gratefully. "Where does a scared and awed probationer report?"

"I'll show you where the Training School Office is," Dr. Clayton said. "Don't know why someone isn't on hand at the information office at the moment. Just leave your suitcase; Willie will bring it over."

Cherry followed his white-clad figure down the quiet corridor. He paused before an attractive office, with T.S.O. printed on the door, where three middle-aged nurses in starched white worked at their desks.

"And here I leave you to your fate," young Dr. Clayton smiled. "See you on the wards." His remark made

Cherry feel awfully professional. Then he strode away.

"Well," Cherry thought, "that's as friendly an introduction to the hospital as anybody could ask." Just the same, her knees threatened to melt under her at the sight of the office. She took a deep steadying breath and walked in.

The nurses looked up, and one of them came forward to greet Cherry.

"I'm Miss Kent, the Assistant Superintendent of Nurses. And you're one of the new probationers, aren't you?"

"I'm Cherry Ames," Cherry gulped. She wondered if new probationers looked peculiar, since everyone could spot them instantly.

"Just a moment. I'll look up your application," Miss Kent said. She leafed through a thick bundle of papers while Cherry prayed nothing would go wrong at this last minute.

"Everything seems to be in order," Miss Kent said. "Next week you will be called down to T.S.O. for a personal interview. Now I'll take you over to Williams Hall. That's the residence for first- and second-year nurses and probationers," Miss Kent explained. Her smile was friendly and reassuring. "Ordinarily we'd go through the yard, but I've an errand to do on the way. So we'll go the long way around."

Cherry followed her, looking respectfully at her hard-won uniform and cap. Miss Kent whisked her through the turns and twists of antiseptic-smelling corridors. Except for a lone interne or a hurrying nurse, there wasn't a soul in sight. As for patients, Cherry thought, apparently the hospital had none. The silence was positively eerie.

"You'll soon learn to find your way through all this labyrinth," Miss Kent said encouragingly. "It seems roundabout to you now, but once you're nursing, you'll find this layout is most convenient in the end."

Cherry was sure she would never remember any of it. Her errand finished, Miss Kent pushed through a door and they walked rapidly across a landscaped lawn. Cherry saw tennis courts in the distance. She had to trot to keep up with the nurse's brisk pace.

Miss Kent pointed out several wings of the hospital. "ENT—GYN—the various O.R.'s—" Cherry's face changed at this strange new language. Miss Kent explained. "Ear, Nose and Throat—Gynecologic—Operating Rooms. You can't see all the buildings from here. The hospital has about fifty-five wards in all, not counting the blood bank and the clinics."

"Golly!" Cherry exclaimed before she realized it was the wrong answer. But Miss Kent only smiled. Cherry did not know where to look first. She looked chiefly at the assistant superintendent's cap, which fascinated her. It was a dainty charlotte russe affair of fluted organdy, and above Miss Kent's rather stern face and muscular figure, it looked strangely frivolous.

Cherry followed Miss Kent and her cap into a large attractive red brick building. Several girls in probationers' gray, and other student nurses in striped blue and white, with crackling white aprons, thronged about the bulletin board and the sitting room on the main floor. Cherry noticed that the humble probationers had no bibs on their aprons and no caps on their heads. After being a mighty senior in high school, here she was a freshman again!

An elevator took them upstairs and after more silent corridors and more mysterious rooms, they paused before an open door.

"And now," Miss Kent said, "this is your room, Miss Ames. Dinner at six. Not in uniform just yet. Probationers' meeting after dinner in Spencer Lounge." She smiled, and vanished on noiseless rubber heels.

Here she was at last!

Cherry started to look around her new room. But she turned as she heard the first sounds since she had entered this quiet place. Girls walked by her door, looking in shyly as if they wanted somebody to talk to. Across the corridor came the splashing of bath water. But first, Cherry decided, she wanted to get herself settled.

It was a darling room, small, but complete and attractive, and all hers. A maple day bed with a luxuriously good mattress, a chest of drawers with a mirror, and a desk also in maple, were arranged against the pale green walls Couch cover and matching curtains were of gay chintz. Two chairs looked inviting, but Cherry suspected she would be too busy to spend much time in them. She went toward the window and stumbled over her suitcase in the center of the cozy little room.

It certainly did not seem like the same suitcase she had packed with Midge's dubious assistance in her own room at home, long ago this morning. Nor did she feel like the same girl. But after Cherry had placed a few of her own things around—photographs of the family and her toilet articles on the dresser, a few of her favorite books on the table beside the day bed —she began to feel completely at home.

The voices in the hall sounded inviting, and Cherry longed to share her excitement with someone who was just as strange and bewildered as she. A few girls poked their heads in, and one freckled face called a friendly "Hello." But Cherry decided she had better rescue her clothes from the suitcase first. Getting everything hung away in the closet or neatly arranged in the chest of drawers took a surprisingly long time. Cherry had not any too much time to bathe in one of the roomy bathrooms and wiggle back into her red suit and a fresh white blouse. By the time she had brushed her dark curls and tried to tone down her rosy cheeks with a little face powder, it was nearly six. Cherry opened her door. All the voices and footsteps had gone. She was all alone on this floor and perhaps in the whole building. She looked about in bewilderment for the right elevator or the right stairs.

"How can I ever find my way back through that wilderness of halls?" she muttered. "I'll probably starve to death. They'll find my body when they return, stuffed with dinner, the wretches."

She walked toward the end of the corridor and boldly went into the first door that looked promising. She found herself in a huge linen closet, with sheets and blankets and towels stacked in neat V's. Cherry backed out and headed for a glass door that might lead to stairs. It led down a short corridor and to another door. Without thinking to knock, Cherry walked in. A very drowsy nurse was just climbing out of bed.

"I—I beg your pardon," Cherry gasped. "I thought you were the way out."

The nurse shook her tousled hair out of her eyes and peered at Cherry. "I am on my way out. To night duty, via second dinner. You're a probationer and you're trying to find first dinner I suppose?"

Cherry nodded miserably. Probationers *were* peculiar-looking, it seemed. Despite her anxiety to get to the dining room on time, she was impressed with the thought of night duty.

"—down these stairs, through the lobby, across the lawn, and first door to your right in Spencer," the nurse was saying. "Not even a probie can miss it. Anyway, you couldn't stay lost long—a searching party could always locate those red cheeks."

"Well, thank you very much," Cherry said uncertainly and flew down the stairs.

"Don't ever get lost in Surgical," the unknown night nurse called after her. "Dr. Wylie won't stand for any nonsense in his ward! And he practically eats student nurses alive!"

Cherry was not sure whether or not she was being teased. But she tucked the name, Dr. Wylie, under the W's in her mind for future reference. She walked across the lawn, cool and dark now in the early dusk, and found her way into Spencer. Troops of nurses were entering the dining room. Cherry entered with them, and stood a moment before the sea of uniforms and tables.

Standing beside Cherry was a poised girl with smooth light brown hair and dark blue eyes. She was about Cherry's age, and she, too, was wearing a traveling suit, of navy blue.

"It's so crowded, guess we'll have to eat standing up, like the cows and the horses," the girl observed. Her voice was quiet, with an undertone of humor. She had a familiar midwest accent, and Cherry smiled at that.

"I'm just as lost around here as you are," Cherry said. "Let's see if we can't find two places together."

They filled their trays at the tempting food counter and wandered about the big pleasant dining room, with its fresh green and peach color scheme. There were tables for four and tables for eight. A big table along the wall was crowded with agonizingly stiff probationers who had apparently drifted together out of their common timidity. But at all the other tables there was much talking and laughter, and there swept over Cherry, from this chattering room and these brisk nurses, a great surge of energy. All these young women in uniform were thoroughly alive, even those tired from just coming off duty. All of them were eager and alert and purposeful, keyed high for action. Already Cherry felt she belonged. But Cherry and her new-found companion did not venture to sit down with the blue-and-white striped student nurses, much less with the white-clad nurses. Though later they learned that probationers were allowed to sit with student nurses, while the graduate nurses shared their tables with the seniors. They finally found a little table tucked in a corner.

Cherry introduced herself. "I'm from Hilton," she added.

"That's close to home!" the other girl said. She held out her hand and Cherry noticed that she too wore a brand-new nurses's watch. "Ann Evans. From Indian City. We probably know loads of the same people."

It turned out that Ann Evans knew Cherry's brother. She had met him at a party.

"I remember dancing with Charles," Ann said, as they ate. "I liked him a lot, except that he more or less ruined my feet. And he talked a lot about flying."

Cherry laughed and nodded. "That's my twin brother, all right! He wants to——"

"Your twin! But he's so blonde!"

"Nobody believes it. We ought to go around with proof. But Dr. Joe can tell you—" She stopped suddenly. Somehow, she did not want to talk about Dr. Joe. Putting aside their empty soup cups and starting on their roast beef made a convenient little interruption. Cherry noticed appreciatively that they were having a good dinner.

Ann's clear cool voice went on talking about her new room. They found that they were on different floors of the Nurses' Residence, but Ann promised to come down and visit the next day. Cherry liked Ann Evans. By the time they came to dessert and coffee, they had really become acquainted. Cherry thought, however, that Ann was rather quiet and serious for a girl her age.

After dinner they looked in at the library with its warm lamps, deep leather sofas and chairs, and up-to-date books and magazines of all kinds.

"Just let me loose in there," Ann said longingly.

"The Superintendent of Nurses comes first," Cherry reminded her. "You know Miss Reamer can't speak until *we* arrive!"

The two girls walked on past the formal and charming reception room, with its wood-paneled walls, to the big sitting room. The new probationers already filled the comfortable sofas and chairs and others were clustered around the huge fireplace. Cherry noticed more books, desks, and a radio-victrola here. But she was more interested in her new classmates. There were about sixty of them—tall girls, short girls, thin, fat, but all of them radiating eagerness and expectancy. Cherry's attention was caught by a girl near by whose cold eyes and overrouged mouth did not seem to belong here.

"I'm Vivian Warren," Cherry heard her say to a plump girl who was placidly eating chocolates from a paper bag.

"My name's Bertha Larsen," the plump girl said. She generously passed over the candy, and urged the stranger to share it.

Cherry saw Vivian's look of amusement and scorn as she helped herself to the other girl's candy. Vivian then rose and without a word left Bertha to herself. The roly-poly girl looked after her, puzzled and hurt.

Cherry felt a quick wave of anger, although she knew it was no concern of hers. She had an idea that she and Vivian Warren were not going to be bosom friends. Ann had seen the little incident, too.

Cherry shook her head and her dark curls danced. "Unfortunately, she'll probably turn out to be one of those terribly efficient nurses—instead of flunking out. What makes people so rude, I wonder?"

"I wonder, too," Ann said thoughtfully.

A burst of laughter came from the other side of the room. Cherry saw a group of girls intent on someone in the center of their circle and she saw a flash of red hair, then heard another peal of laughter. She wondered who the clowning redhead was.

Sitting alone just outside this group, and watching them with a smile, was a slender delicate-looking Chinese girl. She wore a simple black dress, not the traditional long, narrow silk robe, and her satiny black hair was cut short. Her lovely ivory face was marked with the look of tragedy, thought Cherry, though she could be no older than herself.

Suddenly the circle opened, the red hair flashed, and Cherry and Ann caught sight of a snub-nosed face sprinkled with freckles. Cherry recognized it as the face that had popped in cheerfully at her door that afternoon. The redhead bounded toward the Chinese girl. Not even that subdued ivory face could help laughing back into the redhead's gleeful blue eyes.

"We need one more!" she announced and without any further ceremony drew the astonished and pleased Chinese girl into the group. "Can you act?"

"I don't know—I never—" the girl in black said hesitantly, but she disappeared gratefully into the circle. Cherry and Ann looked on fascinated.

"We certainly have a variety of human beings in our class, haven't we?" Cherry commented.

Ann laughed. "By the week end, we'll probably

all be as well acquainted as with our own families."

At that moment a tall middle-aged woman in a rustling white uniform came into the lounge. She had such authority in her bearing that the girls instinctively rose to their feet. She smiled at all of them warmly out of keen gray eyes as she made her way to the front of the sitting room.

Miss Reamer, the Superintendent of Nurses, introduced herself, welcomed the probationers and asked them to be seated. Her face and voice were matter-of-fact. But Cherry discerned in this businesslike woman the same seriousness she respected so deeply in Dr. Joe. Miss Reamer started by telling them that from now on, they were professional women, and that their personal behaviour must reflect the dignity of their profession.

"The first duty of a nurse," the superintendent said slowly and deliberately, "is always to her patient." The words sank in and Cherry knew she would never forget them. She wondered, though, how completely she could forget or sacrifice herself for her patient, or how her dream of being a nurse would stand up under the grim realities of hospital life.

Miss Reamer went on to tell them the history of the great hospital—"my hospital," Cherry thought—and its long tradition of helping the suffering and the needy. Spencer nurses were scattered in all far places of the world, doing their life-bringing work, sometimes in the fire of the battlefields, blazing a path around the globe against pain and death. The girls in the room stirred as she spoke.

"Your own first steps toward a nurse's skill—and toward the coveted nurse's cap," Miss Reamer said, "will be classes. But not for long." They would learn hospital routine gradually on the wards, then more and more, until each student nurse would be responsible for her own patients. Cherry noticed the redheaded girl's face shine at the words, "your own patients," and she herself felt pretty excited at the prospect. ". . . different shifts until you are nursing around the clock," Miss Reamer was saying. Cherry thought of the night nurse whose room she had stumbled into. Soon she would be the lone nurse in charge of twenty or thirty helpless people all night long on a sleeping ward. She glanced at Ann and together they blew out big, half-humorous sighs.

Now the Superintendent was giving them the rules. As nurses, they would rise in the presence of doctors and graduate nurses, in respect to their profession. Nurses' relations with internes—"like Jim Clayton, for instance," Cherry grinned to herself—were to be purely professional. Nurses were not to wander around the hospital but go only to the wards assigned. Nurses must not wear their uniforms or caps on the street, nor wear street clothes on the ward. Miss Reamer recommended a thick white sweater for night duty. No jewelry, no high heels. Several pairs of feet were hastily tucked under chairs.

"As for caps," the Superintendent said with a smile, "if you can pass the three months' probationary period, you will win your cap. Then you will be full-fledged student nurses. Let me remind you that you are going to need good health, intelligence, unselfishness, patience, tact, humor, sympathy, efficiency, neatness, plus plenty of energy for hard work." A groan echoed around the room. "But let me remind you, too," Miss Reamer said, "that nursing is the most rewarding of all professions for women. And frequently the most romantic and exciting," she added with a twinkle. She rose and the probationers rose to their feet with her. "The best of luck to all of you," the Superintendent concluded. "You look to me to have the makings of an exceptionally fine class."

The moment after Miss Reamer had left, the room filled with laughter and moans and a buzz of talk. "An exceptionally fine class, she said!" . . . "Boy, are we going to have to work!" . . . "But the caps are so darling, it's worth it." . . . "I thought all superintendents were slave drivers but she's actually human!" . . . "Gosh, I haven't got all those nurse's virtues!"

"Uniforms tomorrow and my apron *still* slides around!" . . . "Wonder how the internes like that rule."

Cherry and Ann picked their way through the

milling girls in Spencer lobby to the bulletin board where the hospital listed general announcements. Miss Reamer had told them that T.S.O. posted their class schedules, rules, and special announcements on the bulletin board in the Nurses' Residence. Several nurses in blue and white were also studying the Spencer bulletin board. Other members of the new class came up, too, keeping an awed distance from the older nurses.

Suddenly, from around the bend of the corridor, they heard a peculiar sort of explosion. A door shut so violently that one of the blue-clad nurses ran to catch the teetering water cooler. A man's gruff angry voice, and many rapid footsteps, approached them.

"Better duck, kids!" one of the student nurses whispered. "It's the Old Man and he's in battle formation!"

There was no place to duck. A short but imperious man bore down upon them. His long surgeon's coat flapped about his legs, and three nervous internes and two terrified nurses hurried in his wake. He had a sharply intelligent face, with a hawk nose, a jutting square jaw, and a thin mouth tightly clamped shut. The student nurses and the puzzled probationers vainly tried to make themselves inconspicuous. His piercing eyes took in every last detail.

"What are you doing here after ten?" he roared at them, although actually his gruff voice was pitched low. "Childish irresponsible students—get more impossible with each generation!"

He must be pretty important, Cherry thought, for even the two R.N.'s who were standing near by looked troubled. Then, unfortunately, his scowling gaze shifted to Cherry. She wished in terror that she could vanish in a puff of smoke and wondered what she had done. The doctor stared at her fixedly for a long terrible minute of absolute silence.

"Wipe that rouge off your face!" he ordered. All eyes turned fearfully to Cherry. "Soap and water. Good Lord, what is this hospital coming to?"

She said faintly, "I can't wash it off, sir, it's——"

"No impertinence, if you don't mind, young woman!" The doctor turned red in the face. He looked at Cherry as if memorizing her face, then walked on.

It should have been funny but no one laughed. Cherry was trembling. In an irrelevant flash of attention she saw Vivian Warren, carefully expressionless, but with a hint of malicious pleasure about her too red mouth. An older nurse came up to Cherry. She said gravely,

"It's too bad that happened, youngster. He'll remember you."

"Who is he?" Cherry asked innocently, and all the shaken probationers seemed to be breathing the same question down the back of her neck.

"You don't know? You poor kids," said one of the two R.N.'s. "That's Dr. Wylie, Head Resident Surgeon and one of the administrators of the hospital. That's all."

So this was the man the night nurse had warned Cherry about. Other probationers coming out of the lounge asked, "What's the matter?" and fell silent too. The other graduate nurse turned to Cherry. "You'd better get that rouge off. And leave it off."

"But it isn't rouge!" Cherry wailed. "It's me!"

Someone laughed, and it set them all off like a string of firecrackers. They laughed hysterically, even—or especially—Cherry. The two graduate nurses did not join in the laughter. One of them said in sepulchral tones:

"You'll never be able to convince Dr. Wylie that it isn't rouge. He'll merely think you are disobeying his orders."

Ann linked her arm through Cherry's, and the redhead, surprisingly sobered, bobbed up on the other side of her. A sort of funeral guard accompanied Cherry across the black lawn to their residence hall.

"Maybe you ought to carry me back on a stretcher," Cherry said.

"Never mind the old terror," the redhead said under her breath. "A humble probie won't be hobnobbing with the mighty surgeon."

And Ann said, "It's unfortunate but, after all, a surgeon has more important things to worry about."

By the time they had gone up the elevator and trooped through the upstairs corridor, Cherry was laughing at the incident, but there was a persistent little gnawing at the back of her mind. "Silly!" she told herself. "Worrying over a comical mistake. Why, look, it's made me the belle of the class!"

At Cherry's door most of the girls said good night and went chattering off to their own rooms, but Ann and the redhead waited. To Cherry's surprise, she saw the little Chinese girl lingering in the corridor. Cherry turned to invite her in, but she shyly slipped away.

"You mustn't worry about—" Ann said, and at the same instant, the redhead said, "Don't you worry about——"

Cherry stared at them and all three girls burst out laughing. "That's nice of you," Cherry said warmly. "Anyhow, I'm too dazzled with Spencer to waste any time worrying."

"So am I," said the redhead. "Also excited and scared."

Ann nodded agreement in her calm way.

"So scared, in fact," the redhead continued, "that now I wonder why I ever wanted to be a nurse!"

"Why did you?" Cherry asked practically. "Come on in, you two, and we'll——"

"Not tonight you won't," said a smiling student nurse behind them. "Sorry, children, but it's lights out. I'm the Student Organization proctor and you'd better scamper."

"Oh, too bad." They all three looked disappointed.

"Have to make it tomorrow. Think we'll recognize each other in our uniforms?"

"See you at breakfast—if I can pry my eyes open."

"My gosh, classes and stuff tomorrow!"

"Good night!"

"Good night—Nurse!"

Ann vanished down the stairs. The redhead turned halfway down the hall and hissed back at Cherry, "Have you a name?"

Cherry was startled before she laughed and whispered back.

"I'm Gwen Jones and would you please pin down my uniform collar in the morning? It just won't stay down."

"I'm an expert pinner. Bring your problems to—" Cherry saw the proctor coming and ducked into her room. Well, she had two friends already. That was a good start.

She did not remember falling asleep. With her head lying on a strange pillow and not quite recognizing this shadowy room, Cherry felt too excited to sleep. Far away she heard an ambulance gong. Then it seemed that young Dr. Clayton and the Superintendent of Nurses hopped from the ambulance and went off in search of Dr. Wylie, who was furiously roller skating up and down the hospital corridors in pursuit of Cherry's whole class of probationers. Cherry opened her eyes and sat straight up. She had been so sleepy she had forgotten to open her window.

She tiptoed across the moonlit room—the room that was to be hers for the coming year—opened the window and leaned out. The great white hospital buildings gleamed in the darkness. She remembered, after all, the various wings Miss Kent had pointed out to her. Here and there a window glowed softly where nurses kept watch through the night. Over to the right, a whole ground floor blazed brilliantly and Cherry saw tiny figures moving in what she realized must be Emergency Ward. Muffled sounds rose from where she guessed the hospital kitchens were. A single laboratory window shone out steadfastly, as some patient researcher worked. The windows of several operating rooms were alight. The hospital throbbed all about her.

Cherry took a deep breath and slipped back into bed.

"This is the most wonderful thing that ever happened to me," she thought.

CHAPTER III

Miss Mac

THE RISING BELL CLANGED AND CHERRY WOKE UP WITH
a start. One dark eye opened reluctantly and looked at
the clock in a puddle of sunshine on the chest of drawers. Six o'clock. Outside in the corridor Cherry heard
much pattering of footsteps and running water and
sleepy chatter. For a moment she could not think what
all these people were doing in her house. Then she remembered where she was, and leaped out of bed in her
excitement.

"Nurse Ames, on with your uniform!" she told herself. But the uniform, which had fit so neatly at home,
balked under her trembling fingers. And she had to tie
the apron three times before she was satisfied with its
perky bow. She straightened the room and was thinking
of breakfast, when there was a lively knocking on her
door. There stood Ann and Gwen, both of them in their

39

gray dresses with white aprons, and both of them pink with pride and very sleepy.

"We're looking for the girl in the red suit," Gwen announced, peering around.

"She's gone," Cherry laughed back. "Won't Nurse Ames do?"

"How can you joke on empty stomachs?" Ann murmured. "And will you look at that dipping, rolling hem on my dress! Makes me seasick just to gaze upon it."

But they looked at one another's uniforms with admiration. "I think we look elegant," Cherry declared. "We'd gladden the eyes of any patient." However, they pinned and straightened one another before setting out for Spencer and the dining room.

A voice wailed after them. "Oh, wait for me!" They turned to see Bertha Larsen hurrying along, looking untidy in her gray uniform but shining with excitement. "My goodness, but I'm hungry," Bertha Larsen panted. "Breakfast is a whole two hours late for me!"

"Sounds like a farm," said a small pretty blonde girl in the elevator, whom Cherry vaguely remembered from the day before. "Me, I've always had breakfast in bed around noon. And I'm sick and tired of it. Guess we'll breakfast at seven and like it."

Cherry and the other girls looked at her curiously, and saw from her humorously determined little face that she meant what she said. When they entered the dining room, to Cherry's surprise, at least a dozen girls greeted her and joked with her about her cherry cheeks.

"You're practically a celebrity," Ann told her as they sat down at a sunny table.

"A nurse ought to look healthy—good advertisement for the profession," Gwen defended her. "Can you imagine how a patient would feel looking at a sick, gloomy nurse who was barely able to crawl?" She shuddered in mock horror and fell upon her food as if determined that no such thing should ever happen to her.

"I'm going to run, not crawl, if I ever see Dr. Wylie coming," Cherry replied.

Bertha was too busy eating to talk. She looked up only once and said sadly, with her mouth full, "Did you hear? We aren't allowed to eat on the wards! Bet some of the nurses do it, though."

The little blonde girl had drifted to another table. Other girls came up to speak to Cherry. The dining room buzzed with rumors of what their classes and teachers would be like.

"You poor innocents!" called a senior nurse from the next table. "I hope you'll be able to eat your lunch!"

Choruses of bewildered "Why?" "What's so terrible?" echoed around the room. But the night nurses shook their heads pityingly and their shoulders shook with laughter.

"Just wait," they said ominously. "Misplace one

sponge—or put the thermometer back in the wrong place—and T.S.O. will——"

"Maybe we'll do everything right," a timid voice quavered.

"Oh, the poor lambs! Just asking to be slaughtered!"

Cherry rose and fled, with Gwen and Ann right behind her.

"We might as well see the scaffold," Cherry said grimly.

With Gwen humming a mournful tune, the three of them marched in double-slow time to Spencer basement where the classroom was. Their first discovery was a sink.

"Nothing so terrifying about a sink," Cherry said.

They poked their heads inquisitively into the two doors alongside. Here they found a small laboratory and a tiny linen closet.

"They don't terrify me either," Cherry declared.

The rest of the basement, as far as they could see, was a bewildering labyrinth of corridors, pipes, and service rooms.

"You could get lost down here," Ann said.

They marched quite boldly into the classroom. It looked like any classroom, with its chairs each with one wide arm, and its low platform for the teacher's table and chair. But all along one side of the room were beds, perhaps a dozen of them. And on the platform was another bed. Cherry jumped slightly. Someone was in it.

A few other girls, including the Chinese girl and Vivian Warren, her face now discreetly free of excess make-up, were already waiting in their chairs. All eyes were upon the figure in the bed. Whoever it was, it was a mystery how he or she breathed, for the covers were drawn up over its head. Some of the girls looked at it curiously and some smiled knowingly.

Cherry and Ann sat down near the front of the room. Gwen started for the beds. "I could use one of those," she whispered. Laughing, they pulled her into a chair beside them. Gradually the rest of the class trooped in, all solemn and apprehensive. There was an awful five minutes of waiting for an unknown teacher. The probies joked nervously among themselves.

"Maybe that thing in the bed is a corpse," someone whispered in back of Cherry.

Someone else gasped. "Do you really think it is?" Cherry turned around and recognized Josie Franklin, the timid girl with glasses.

A door creaked and light footsteps ran down the stairs. The probationers assumed the look they would wear on Judgment Day and temporarily stopped breathing. When they saw the lively young person who came in, there was a rustle and a sigh as they all relaxed.

Miss McIntyre, the instructor in Nursing Arts, was a brisk, dashing young woman who made you feel that she was tops in efficiency. At the same time she made you think of whirlwind tennis, a sports roadster with a wire-haired terrier hanging out the front seat, and plenty of beaux. In fact, Cherry learned later, until the war Miss McIntyre had had her roadster, as well as her own apartment, when she wasn't driving from one end of the United States to the other on private cases. As she swung up onto the platform, the probationers noticed she wore her white uniform like a stunning sports dress, and that her nurse's cap, with the wide black velvet band of the graduate, sat astride a rakish brown bob. She was just the sort of person the girls would refer to affectionately as "Miss Mac"—and Cherry soon learned she was called just that.

She called the roll at furious speed, looking for each girl's face, and though she grinned at them, there was no nonsense about her. "I'll bet that with her, you've got to get it right the first time, and quick," Cherry whispered to Ann.

Ann scribbled back on the margin of her notebook, "T.S.O. takes *her* word for whether you win your cap or not." Cherry blinked and passed the note on to Gwen.

Miss McIntyre perched herself on the edge of her table and shot at them, "This isn't conventional, but I want to know. Why do you want to be nurses?"

The girls sat up startled. Miss Mac held the roll in her hand. "Miss Franklin. Come on now, speak up," she said crisply.

Josie Franklin stood up. She opened her mouth but

no sound came out. "Let's hear the worst," Miss Mac's voice was encouraging. The girls all laughed—even Josie, who began bravely,

"I guess I always wanted to be a nurse. When I played with dolls, they were always patients. And I was always fixing up dogs or birds or cats in our neighborhood that got hurt, or binding up my kid sister's bumps. I guess I just—well, I can't help it! I just *want* to take care of people."

"That's an excellent attitude," Miss McIntyre said. "Some of us are born nurses."

Cherry did a little hasty soul-searching. She didn't think she had been born anything in particular. Good grief, what was she going to say for herself? Would Miss McIntyre understand about Dr. Joe? But she forgot to worry as Miss McIntyre called out, "Miss Jones!" and poor Gwen stood up. She was right beside Cherry and Cherry could feel her shaking.

"Well, my Dad's a doctor, an industrial doctor in a coal mining town. I've seen accidents and sickness and children born, and I know the great need for doctors and nurses." Cherry looked up at her in surprise. Suddenly Gwen tossed her red head and her usual gaiety returned. "And living in a medical household means never a dull moment. I like people and it's fun to be dealing with them all the time."

"Miss Jones obviously knows whereof she speaks,"

Miss McIntyre said. "Next! Miss— Let's see. Miss Swift." The little blonde who until today had breakfasted in bed stood up.

"I want to do something useful. I've found out that if you don't, you're bored and discontented and even lonesome. And I can't think of anything more useful than nursing."

Miss McIntyre nodded. "Miss Evans!"

Ann rose. She was calm but Cherry saw that her face was curiously strained. "My father was maimed in the last war. He would not be lame today if there had been enough nurses to send even one into the area where he was. And now—" Ann swallowed but went on quietly, "my two older brothers and my fiancé have enlisted. I'm going to be an Army nurse." She sat down abruptly.

Everybody tactfully avoided staring at her.

Suddenly the Chinese girl was on her feet, speaking —and speaking directly to Ann. "I am going to be an Army nurse, too. My family, my town—I beg your pardon, Miss McIntyre," she apologized, looking at the instructor with pleading almond eyes, "but may I please speak next? My name is Mai Lee. I was born in this country but my family is in China. Two years ago I went back to see them and see the village where my ancestors have always lived in peace." Her ivory face was impassive but her voice shook. "When I had been there five days, Japanese planes bombed our little village." Her small hands gripped the back of the chair before her. "My family was killed, the village isn't there any more. But I'm going to learn to be a nurse and I'm going back." She seated herself with fierce, quiet dignity.

There was a moment's stunned silence. Suddenly the room burst into applause. Cherry felt hot tears sting her eyes.

"I congratulate you on your courage," Miss McIntyre said to Mai Lee, and she glanced understandingly at Ann, too. "I expect that many of you will answer the Army's call for nurses."

She stood up and put the roll away. "You are too large a class for all of you to introduce yourselves today," Miss McIntyre explained. "More next time. And now let's get down to business."

The class, feeling better acquainted, lined up at the back of the room for a rapid inspection of uniforms. Miss Mac raced down the line, tossing out orders: "Your collar's untidy. Get rid of that fancy hair-do. Buy flat-heeled shoes this afternoon. Shorten your apron. Sewing room on the second floor of Spencer. A nurse must be neat as a pin! Over to the supply closet now!" The class hustled after her brisk steps. Keeping up with her left them a little breathless.

Miss Mac opened the door of the closet, which contained bandages, tape, scissors, twine, rubber sheets, and a collection of other things. "Same as on the wards. Memorize it. Everything must always be in the same place." The class stared but already she was whisking them along to the laboratory.

"I heard that if you even put the bandages back in the wrong place, you get expelled," Josie Franklin whispered to Cherry as they hurried after Miss McIntyre.

"That must be what happened to the poor soul in bed on the platform," Cherry whispered back. Miss Franklin looked decidedly uncomfortable.

Miss Mac had flung open the door of the laboratory closet. Its huge five-pint bottles of antiseptics gleaming blue, green, yellow, and red reminded Cherry of the jars in apothecary's windows. Above them on a shelf were rubber gloves and rubber tubing. Surgical instruments, if the class needed them, would be borrowed from the wards. Poultice pans stood in copper racks. "You'll memorize this," Miss Mac said casually. "And memorize the linen closet," she added, opening that door too. The class felt stunned.

"She's so good herself, she thinks we're wonders too," Cherry thought. But she realized that practice in class would thoroughly familiarize her with the contents of those closets.

When they were back in their seats, Miss McIntyre distributed notebooks and instructed them in rapid succession on how to clean a room and how to keep an icebox sanitary. While they were still digesting this, she proceeded to bedmaking. "I'll need an assistant," Miss Mac said. She consulted the roll. "Miss Ames."

"Go on up," Gwen whispered. "The corpse needs you."

Cherry trotted up to the platform uncertainly.

"Hello, Miss Ames," said Miss Mac with a nice smile. "Will you lift up the patient?"

The class watched with a suspicion of a grin.

Cherry reached for the still figure. It was cold and clammy and surprisingly light. Then she pulled back the sheet from its face and almost laughed. It was a doll, a rubber doll with a giddy painted smile and eyes that went off in independent directions. It had a humorously resigned look—from long suffering, Cherry supposed. Cherry held it up wickedly before the class.

"This is Sally Chase, the demonstration doll," Miss Mac said. The class nodded very wisely and professionally. Miss McIntyre started to make the bed. "You pull the sheet taut so that it cannot wrinkle, and fold square corners, at right angles, and press in tight, so the covers cannot slip. You make first one side of the bed, then the other, without disturbing your patient." She showed them the rubber sheet, which was about two feet wide and went across the middle of the bed, over the bottom sheet. Then came the draw sheet. "This is the way you'll do it on the wards. First, you will practice making empty beds, then with the doll in it, then with a student patient it it."

Cherry assisted a little. When Miss McIntyre was finished she thanked Cherry and said, "You have a light hand and you didn't bump against the bed. That's important, class. Sick people don't enjoy an elephant thumping around." Sally Chase, too, seemed to smile her foolish satisfaction.

Then Miss McIntyre announced, with a straight face but with laughter in her eyes, that for the first month they would practice what they learned here in Nursing Arts class—feeding and bathing patients, giving hypodermics—on one another. A subdued giggle ran around the room as the girls, all too vividly, visualized feeding and being fed by their fellow probies. Miss Mac tried to look stern as she added, "You will practice on your 'patients' in this classroom and I will also give you assignments, such as bed baths, to be done in your own rooms."

At that, Cherry dared not glance at Gwen, whose shoulders were shaking.

After a quick demonstration of taking temperatures, and a few more instructions on the rest of the day's routine, Miss McIntyre dismissed them. They surged on to their other classes, chattering on the way.

"The nicer they are, the tougher they are," someone predicted gloomily.

Josie Franklin was exclaiming to anyone who would listen to her, "Only a doll! Why, I thought I'd collapse."

Bertha Larsen wailed, "Memorize three closets with a million things in them, just like it was nothing!"

Cherry and Ann and Gwen listened to the talk

around them, and grinned their amusement at one another. Ann said thoughtfully, "Wonder if we'll be on
ward duty together by any chance? I don't suppose
T.S.O. would arrange it for us. But we can take our
time off duty together."

Gwen said heartily, "I'm looking forward to ward
duty with Mai Lee. Imagine that spunky little thing!"

Cherry had her mouth open to reply when she heard
Vivian Warren's voice in an undertone. "She likes that
Ames," Vivian was saying. "You can just *see* it." That
was all Cherry could hear, for by then they had reached
the classroom.

The rest of their classes turned out to be an anatomy
and physiology class, plus a class in therapeutics or the
study of the effects of different medicines. Hard on the
heels of these classes came mental tests, which reminded
Cherry irreverently of playing games. Then thorough
physical examinations—tonsils, teeth, chest X-rays,
everything. Cherry did not mind, for she knew that if
a nurse was to heal the sick, she herself had to have
good stout health. The probationers were given im-
munization against certain contagious diseases and a
lecture on scientific precautions they must take in the
sickroom. "You young ladies are going to grow taller
and rounder and stronger here," the doctor told them,
"because you will have a regular routine and a well-
balanced diet and exercise in the gymnasium. And early
to bed," he added with a smile. He told them that they

would receive frequent physical check-ups and, should they ever need it, immediate care.

Then they went back to the dining room, ravenous.

"I'm so stuffed with knowledge I feel like an overcooked sausage who's going to burst out of its skin!" Cherry confided to Ann at lunch.

"Sausages aren't stuffed with knowledge," Ann said with a straight face. "I'll ask T.S.O. to arrange a sausage class for you, too."

"Not so different from high school, is it?" Gwen said over the rim of her glass of milk. "Except that teacher wears a nurse's uniform and we're all expected to be mental marvels. I'm going to give up sleeping and just *memorize!*"

They finished lunch and hurried out to the bulletin board. The class had been divided ("like Gaul, girls," Ann said) into three sections. To their delight, the three of them were in the same section. Beside their names on the bulletin board were the numbers of wards, which might as well have been the Secret of the Ages to them. Cherry was to be assigned to Ward 4 and Josie Franklin was on Ward 4 with her. Gwen and Ann each were going to go on different wards. Ann had drawn a Miss P. Shore, a totally unknown quantity. Bertha Larsen, Cherry noted, would have Vivian Warren to work with. Cherry hoped that good-natured Bertha would find the right way to get along with her. Gwen did not know Miss S. Stevenson, the probationer who was going with her to Ward 23.

"What the dickens is Ward 4?" Cherry wondered aloud.

"Whatever Ward 17 turns out to be," Ann declared, "I'm excited!"

Gwen was almost dancing in her hurry to do some actual nursing. "Think they'll let me change a dressing? Too soon? Maybe they'll let me take off a plaster cast!"

A passing student head nurse said haughtily, "They *may* trust you to go for clean towels, until you learn something."

Gwen was mimicking the nurse's self-important walk when the nurse turned around and said, "Don't be too elated over ward duty. You won't have it for a month yet—until, as I said before, you learn something!"

"What!" they exclaimed in a disappointed chorus.

Gwen raced back to the bulletin board and put one finger on the date. "She's right—worse luck. A whole month to wait!"

Their faces fell.

"I suppose," Ann said evenly, "that's posted now so we'll have a chance to get acquainted with the girls we're to work with. Maybe it's to encourage us in our class studies, too."

"It certainly encourages me," Cherry said. She took a deep breath. "Well, a month is only thirty days."

CHAPTER IV

Nurse! Nurse!

BY THE TIME WARD DUTY ARRIVED, CHERRY'S EXCITE-ment had become tempered with nervousness. Climb-ing up the stairs to Ward 4, on the first of October, she had some extremely gloomy ideas. Just outside the ward door, she met Josie Franklin. Josie was pale, earnest, and perspiring. She whole-heartedly expected to do all the wrong things.

"You'll never do the right things in that state of mind," Cherry assured her. She took Josie's hand, and with a boldness she did not feel, half pushed and half dragged Josie to the door of Ward 4.

Cherry stood on the threshold and tried to see every-thing in the ward in one excited glance. There was a great deal to see, and everything was in beautiful order. ᵀt was a large room, warm and sunny and quiet, with rows and rows of white beds along the walls. Some of the women patients lay very still in their beds. A few sat stiffly in chairs around an oak table and listened to the ward radio. But most of the patients, here on Women's Medical, were walking gingerly about in bathrobes, chatting and looking out the windows. The ward had a friendly, peaceful atmosphere, although behind it Cherry sensed the whole great hospital organization firmly at work.

Near the door was a desk—the head nurse's desk. Cherry knew, from its location, that the sickest patients were closest to the desk and whoever had the beds nearest the far windows were almost well. In fact, almost all the patients were nearly well. "Guess T.S.O. doesn't trust probies with really sick people," Cherry thought, and felt about one inch tall. Behind her, Josie Franklin was grabbing at her apron tails.

"Well, come *on!*" Cherry said and walked into the quiet ward to report to the head nurse. Josie was right behind her.

A young graduate nurse came down the row of beds to greet them. "I'm Miss Baker, the head nurse on Ward 4," she said. She was pretty, with candid hazel eyes and a mass of soft blonde hair. Miss Baker was so young that Cherry thought the graduate's wide black velvet ribbon on her cap must be very recent indeed. "You're Miss Ames and Miss Franklin—but which of you is which?"

The probationers introduced themselves.

"Well, I'm very glad to have you on my ward."

Cherry was relieved to hear that. She'd heard at lunch that head nurses, particularly young new ones, considered green probationers just a nuisance. Out of the corner of her eye, Cherry saw that Josie had lost that hunted rabbit look.

"I want you to meet Miss Antonio and Miss Prentice, the other nurses on this ward."

These were two older student nurses in striped blue and white. Miss Antonio, a short dark girl who was encouraging a patient to eat, looked up and smiled understandingly. Tall, chilly Miss Prentice, with her arms full of dinner trays, nodded without much interest.

"Now—uh—let's see what you can do to help," the pretty head nurse said thoughtfully. Cherry saw at once that student nurses never make a move except under close and continual supervision. "Miss Franklin, would you get clean towels from the linen closet?" Cherry swallowed a giggle. Just what the insulting nurse had predicted a month ago! But Miss Baker, with her clear eyes and friendly voice, put it so nicely. "We've been needing clean towels all morning and no one's had a chance to get them." Miss Franklin rushed off, eager and confident.

"What a darling Miss Baker is," Cherry thought. "If she asked me to scrub the floor with a toothbrush, I believe I'd say 'Thank you!' "

"And you, Miss Ames. I think Miss Prentice could use some help in the kitchen. The ward's just had lunch, you know."

Cherry went into the kitchen rather disappointed, for she wanted to stay on the ward and get to know the patients. She had daydreamed a bit about how her presence on the ward might bring untold comfort to the sick.

But the tiny kitchen was fun in its way, even though she and Miss Prentice stepped on each other's toes as they stacked trays. It was clear that Miss Prentice considered probationers less than nothing. "She acts as if she was never a probie herself," Cherry thought. "Maybe she sprang from the cradle direct to student nurse." She was puzzled by the chevrons on her student nurse's uniform. With careful respect, she asked Miss Prentice what they stood for.

Miss Prentice peered down from the heights of her dignity, rather flattered. "That's because I'm a third year nurse. Also, I've been on Ward 4 longer than any other student nurse, and I'm in charge when Miss Baker is off duty." She seemed to regret her condescension and immediately froze again.

Cherry ignored Miss Prentice in her own turn and put her attention on the ward kitchen. It was tiny but complete, with a sink, steam table, and dumb-waiter. Over the clash of dishes and forks, Miss Prentice—to Cherry's amazement—explained about special diets versus regular house diets. They stacked and stacked for what seemed like hours. Then Miss Antonio shoved in the last of the trays, and suddenly Cherry found that her job had melted away. Miss Prentice hurried off to X-ray. Cherry wandered back into the ward, feeling ignorant and in the way.

"Well, at any rate," she thought, "it doesn't take training to be cheerful and pleasant to the patients. I *know* I could handle them if Miss Baker would just give me the chance."

The chance came immediately. Miss Baker called Cherry over to her desk and said, "Will you see if anyone wants anything, Miss Ames, and see if everyone is comfortable for the afternoon rest?"

Cherry brightened and started down the row of beds. At the first bed she carelessly rested her hand on the patient's table.

"Don't do that!" the gray-haired woman on the pillow exclaimed querulously. "You'll get my bed jacket all wrinkled!"

"I'm sorry," Cherry said. Her hand was nowhere near the pink bed jacket but Cherry thought it wiser not to say so, and obediently moved it away.

"For heaven's sake!" the patient complained. "I don't see why you have to bother me anyhow!"

"Is there anything you'd like?" Cherry asked gently, hanging on tight to her temper. "Are you comfortable?"

"Of course I'm not comfortable. How can I be comfortable with a raging fever and a horrible headache? I suppose you think I'm complaining. Well, I'm sick! I'm sick so I've got a right to complain!"

Miss Antonio came up noiselessly. Cherry felt her cheeks flame as she retreated. With deft strong hands the older nurse drew up the patient's covers and said, "You must try to rest now, Mrs. Brownlee. No more talking." She wheeled and left her, motioning Cherry to leave too. The gray-haired woman started to grumble again but Miss Antonio said firmly, "Time for a nap." And the patient subsided.

With a grin, Cherry thanked Miss Antonio for her lesson in practical psychology. "This is going to take learning," Cherry told herself. "I guess I'm not such a master mind at that." She approached her next patient more cautiously.

A pretty little blonde woman smiled up at her and asked Cherry to pour her a glass of water from the pitcher on her bedside table. Cherry steadied the woman's thin shoulders as she lifted herself to drink. The woman's weakness, and her grateful glance, made Cherry feel very protective.

"Don't you mind that mean ol' Mis' Brownlee, honey," she whispered to Cherry over the rim of her glass. "Don't you worry. You're going to do fine."

Now it was Cherry's turn to be grateful. The soft Southern drawl went on. "Now when you come to that funny Mis' Noonan, down in the bed yonder, b॰

sure you tell her how fine she's looking today. She certainly loves to hear that. And, honey, take care with that fat Mis' Crosser. Don't you bother her. She's a caution for cats." Cherry's lips twitched. She saw that this gossipy, good-hearted little patient would keep her here all day if she was not careful, and a woman in another bed was looking jealously toward her. "That Mis' Brackett, now, she's a sad case, honestly, it's a real pity——"

"Nurse!" came a tired voice from the next bed. "I'm so thirsty—please."

The whisper went on, "*She* always feels neglected, honey. Now if there's the least little thing you want to know, just you come to me. I can see you're new."

Cherry thanked her with mixed emotions and hurried on to the next bed. This pale woman accepted Cherry's help with the glass, drank it all, and lay back listlessly on the pillow without a word. Cherry rearranged her blanket and, seeing how exhausted the patient was, kept silent. The woman thanked her with heavy eyes.

On light feet she went down the row of beds. Across the room, she saw Josie doing the same thing—not a scared Josie now—for she was so absorbed in easing the patients that she had mercifully forgotten herself.

Cherry slowly gathered confidence as most of the women unquestioningly accepted her ministrations. Cherry looked down into the contrasting faces: a plump Jewish grandmother, an Italian woman with a smile like a sunburst, a tiny little Irish girl not much older than herself, a Slavic woman who spoke no English. What an assorted lot they were! And each patient's personality was so different, too; for each one, Cherry had to find a different approach. It was challenging, it was fun. All went well until Cherry came to the last bed.

A stern middle-aged woman glanced at her critically and demanded, "How old are you?"

Cherry jumped. "Eighteen."

"Same's my girl." The woman's mouth shut like a clamp. "Hasn't the sense of a chicken. Too young," she proclaimed loudly enough for the whole ward to hear.

"If you'd turn your head a little—" Cherry suggested, reaching to plump up the twisted pillow, and trying to change the subject.

"Entirely too young to be in a hospital." The woman ignored Cherry's efforts. The other patients were taking an interest. Cherry's gingerly developing confidence did a back flip. "Besides, you don't look a day over fifteen to me."

Cherry was fumbling for her professional authority when Miss Baker came to the rescue. There was an amused look in her clear hazel eyes. "Very good, Miss Ames," she said approvingly, within the patient's hearing. At that moment Cherry could have hugged her. She went off limply into the kitchen.

A moment later, Josie Franklin stumbled into the kitchen, too. She managed to look both frightened and elated. "Isn't it awful?" she panted. "But—I can't believe it—some of them seemed to like me!" She added mournfully, "And some of them didn't."

Cherry nodded as they each sipped a glass of water. "Buck up. After all, it's only our first day on the ward and there's worse coming." Josie looked so gloomy that Cherry exclaimed, "Silly, I'm only teasing!"

"Don't tease me," Josie warned. "I might collapse." She looked at Cherry soberly from behind her glasses. "I'm glad I'm working with you, you're so sure of yourself. *You* aren't a bit scared."

Cherry simply leaned against the sink and laughed.

Miss Baker came in and assigned them several small jobs. Almost all the patients were asleep now, so they had to move softly as they boiled rubber gloves in the fish kettle, a long, low pan shaped like a fish, powdered and tested them for holes and sent them out to be sterilized. The afternoon wore away. They helped the maid put away clean linens and boiled glasses and pitchers in the sterilizer. The head nurse sent Cherry to get a prescription filled. By the time she returned from the apothecary in a distant wing of the hospital, the ward was waking up.

Now Miss Antonio and Miss Prentice were busy taking four o'clock temperatures, respiration and pulse, and noting these on each patient's chart for the interne's visit. Shades were raised, flooding the ward with late afternoon sunlight. Cherry was so busy remaking an empty bed that she did not see the interne come in. But when the man in the white suit talking to Miss Baker turned around, she felt a little tingle of surprise.

The doctor assigned to Women's Medical was young Dr. James Clayton.

Cherry remembered how chivalrous he had been that first day he had found her in the rotunda, and involuntarily she patted her black curls into place. Dr. Clayton looked very tall and young and handsome, in spite of his matter-of-fact professional air as he glanced over the charts. Miss Baker's fair head came only to his shoulder and Cherry thought how romantic these two nice people looked together. However, there was nothing romantic to be seen in their manners—just the dignified impersonal courtesy of doctor and head nurse.

Cherry overheard them say something about "that little Britisher" and she distinctly heard the terrible Dr. Wylie's name. She wondered hopefully if young Dr. Clayton would stop to speak to her. Probably not. After all, this was a hospital ward, not a tea party.

Cherry had not counted on Miss Baker. The head nurse took the trouble to introduce her two new probationers to the ward's house officer. Cherry found herself looking up into Dr. Jim Clayton's dark brown eyes. He said merely, "How do you do," and did not smile, but a current of recognition and friendliness ran between him and Cherry. Cherry felt warmed and grateful and reassured to be made welcome like this, and now she felt a part of the ward with all her heart.

"Isn't he nice!" Josie exclaimed under her breath as they turned away.

The patients seemed to think so, too. Dr. Clayton magically turned each routine check-up into a friendly little visit. However impersonal and hurried he was with the staff, he joked and chatted leisurely with the patients. Cherry saw cross Mrs. Brownlee cease grumbling and look pleasant, and even Mrs. Thompson, the middle-aged woman in the last bed, thawed out under his engaging smile. The whole ward seemed to have perked up. Cherry half envied the patients, for when Dr. Clayton had completed his tour, he turned briefly to Miss Baker, gave a few crisp orders, and strode away. Some of his vitality and warm good spirits seemed to linger in the air, and enliven the ward, even after he had gone.

Before Cherry knew it, it was four-thirty. She and Josie went to Miss Baker to report off duty. The head nurse smiled at them from her desk where she was preparing the day report book for the night nurse.

"Good night, Miss Ames—good night, Miss Franklin. I hope you didn't have too difficult a time of it your first day."

Josie sighed. "It's only my feet that are tired, the rest of me could stay forever, I'm that fascinated."

Cherry said impulsively, "I liked the sample I had today, and I want more."

"Good!" Miss Baker laughed. "You're going to be on Women's Medical for the next month, you know, so I'm glad you feel at home here." She dismissed them with a smile and returned to the day report. Miss Antonio and Miss Prentice were preparing to go off duty, too. Cherry and her companion said good night to them, and went off down the antiseptic-smelling corridor.

"Apron!" Cherry exclaimed as they rounded a corner.

"What apron?" said Josie, trotting along beside her.

"Mine," Cherry explained. "Miss Mac said to shorten it, so I'll just run up to the second floor and see if I can locate the sewing room."

She promised to see Josie at dinner and went off in search of the sewing room. It was quite a long walk, down to another floor, past other wards with their doors tantalizingly ajar, and through a quiet private pavilion. Cherry found the right room at last. The sewing room was not busy, and was so well-equipped that Cherry ran up the hem of her apron in exactly four minutes. Out in the hall again, she started to retrace her steps. She thought she would go down to the lounge and library— Gwen and Ann might be there and Cherry was eager to compare notes on their afternoon's adventures. She glanced at her watch with its spinning second hand. Nearly five. She was off duty until the rising bell tomorrow morning. She would study, and rinse out a few things, Cherry decided, as she walked along through the deserted halls of the private pavilion. She would write a letter home and one to Dr. Joe.

Suddenly she stopped. She forgot her plans. A high thin voice was calling—seemed to be calling her. Certainly there was no one else within sight or sound in this pale green corridor of closed doors. Only one door was open, at the isolated end of the hall. The door of the voice.

It was a remarkable voice, very British, very high-pitched, feeble but imperious. "Nurse! Nurse!" it demanded. "Can't you possibly come? Do come! Nurse!" It sounded to Cherry like the sad voice of an old person.

She looked hastily around. She knew enough of hospital routine to call the floor nurse in charge but her desk, tiny at the far end of the corridor, was deserted. Cherry flew silently down the long hall to the nurses' small sitting room, but its chintz chairs and table with its vase of roses winked emptily back at her. A glimpse at the call board showed her that all the private duty nurses here were busy, and only Room Number One's bell buzzed persistently on the board.

Cherry went back into the hall, and stood looking around. If only somebody would pass by—even a student nurse, an orderly, a maid, anybody. That poor old Britisher in Room One—for that was what Cherry decided the voice was—might be in real trouble.

The voice called again, very faint. Cherry ran toward it. The very least she could do was find out what was wrong and summon help if necessary. She had no right to be in this wing, but was it not a nurse's duty to report an emergency? That poor old Britisher . . . Cherry popped into the private room and gasped.

In the bed lay a tiny girl. She could not have been over six or seven years old. Her pinched little face looked imploringly at Cherry from the pillow, and Cherry saw that the child's leg was enormously bandaged in a plaster cast and raised at a steep angle by a pulley. She was pale and restless. "She must be in pain," Cherry thought, "with that great weight pulling at her hip."

"I say, have you seen my mummy?" the child piped. "I'm dreadfully lonesome for my mummy. I call and call, but she never comes."

"Why, you poor little tyke," Cherry breathed. She moved closer to the bed and saw tear smudges on the child's wan cheeks. "Where is your mother?"

"I haven't seen my mummy since London. I was asleep in the shelter and Jerry came over and I got hurt and I don't know where my mummy is. But the doctor *said* she's coming, so I thought p'rhaps she came today." The little girl looked up at Cherry with trusting eyes. "I daresay she'll be along soon, though. He *said* so."

"Oh," Cherry said. London. Bombings. Perhaps that was why this forlorn scrap of a girl lay half-crippled in a hospital, waiting for a mother who might have been killed. Cherry had read of children and wounded people being evacuated from the Allied countries. But the reality she saw before her now was so cruel it was almost unbearable.

"I came over on a big boat," the child offered conversationally.

Cherry could not talk. She was angry—fighting mad at the bitter evidence she saw before her. She choked in her fury and took the child's hand. The little girl curled her fingers around Cherry's. "I don't feel so lonesome now," she said. "I don't s'pose you could stay here and play with me, could you?"

"No, I have lots of things I must do, you see. But your own nurse will come in and talk to you while you eat your supper."

The child sighed. "She never can stay awfully long either. I say, have you by any chance a doll? I should so like a doll." Cherry glanced around the room and saw blocks, a clumsy toy train and a well-thumbed picture book—but no doll. "That is, if you please, Nurse. A doll wouldn't have to go away and a doll is really quite a lot of company, you know."

Cherry breathed in sharply. "You shall have a doll," she promised.

The little girl's eyes widened. "Truly? Right away?"

"Right away. You just be patient and I'll be right back with a doll."

The little clipped voice followed Cherry joyfully into the hall. "Oh, thank you, thank you, Nurse!"

The corridor was still deserted as Cherry hurried toward the stairs. She hadn't the faintest idea where she was going to get a doll. The children's wing, which was a good two blocks away, might supply one on requisition from the proper hospital authority but that would take days of waiting. Cherry thought fleetingly it was a pity the little girl could not be in the children's ward, instead of alone in a private room, but no doubt her doctor had his reasons. It was too late to go to a store to buy anything today. Cherry thought of making a rag doll out of a knotted towel. But such a crude plaything would not be company for anyone but the tiniest child. Or she could cut out paper dolls. No, it must be a real one. Preferably a big one. Cherry concentrated as she went along downstairs and toward the lounge. Where, where, where was she going to find a doll? She had promised one, she had to produce one.

Suddenly Cherry had an inspiration. Miss Sally Chase. She would borrow Miss Sally Chase.

CHAPTER V

Alias Mona

"BUT YOU CAN'T DO SUCH A THING!" ANN PROTESTED. "You'll be expelled! Cherry Ames, listen to reason!"

"You listen to *me!*" Cherry said. She pulled Ann to a deserted corner of the big lounge. She was still out of breath.

Gwen whirled in at that moment, her freckled face smudged but her grin undaunted. "Why all the mystery?" she whispered loudly, as she came over to their corner.

Ann's calm blue eyes were troubled. "This idiot wants to kidnap Sally Chase."

Gwen looked at Cherry with interest. "Sounds like fun. Want an assistant?"

Ann moaned. "Not so fast. Think of what you're doing. Think of——"

"Think of this," Cherry said tersely. And she told

them about the little English girl. After she had finished, they looked at one another in silence.

Finally Ann said, "Certainly the little girl should have her doll! But can't we wait until tomorrow and buy a doll?"

"That little girl is pitifully lonely," Cherry said. "She's been crying her heart out, all alone in there. How long do you think she can stand it?"

"That poor baby!" Gwen exclaimed. "Come on!"

"But if we take Sally Chase," Ann interrupted, "and get expelled for it, we can't be nurses. Now, please, please, be sensible, you two."

Gwen's red hair seemed to bristle. "I'll be sensible some other time. Right now I want to get that lonely little girl her doll."

"I knew you would," Cherry said delightedly.

Ann resigned herself with a sigh. "All right, count me in."

"I knew you would too," Cherry teased her. The three of them smiled at one another in perfect understanding. "Anyhow, it'll be cozy getting expelled together. And now let's work out a plan. We haven't much time before dinner, and that child is waiting for us."

The three girls retired deeper into the corner and whispered earnestly. Then Ann hastily disappeared toward the Nurses' Residence while Cherry and Gwen waited. Soon Ann reappeared with a flowered silk house-coat and matching slippers and a big pink chiffon scarf, and handed them over. Then she slipped up the stairs toward the private pavilion. Cherry and Gwen melted away down the stairs to the basement. The halls were empty at this hour; the ward shifts had changed over an hour before. The nurses who were not on ward duty were in their rooms resting and changing before dinner. Staff doctors—except for emergencies—were in offices or laboratories finishing up for the day, and night doctors had not yet come on. Most important of all, Cherry had learned from the bulletin board that morning that the private duty nurses—which would include the little girl's nurse—would be attending a lecture by a visiting psychologist at this time. Only a few relief nurses would be left on the private pavilion for a while. The coast was clear, and Cherry prayed it would stay that way.

In the shadowy basement, Cherry, with Gwen on her heels, eased open the door of Miss Mac's classroom. The blue light of evening fell eerily on their empty one-armed chairs and on the empty demonstration beds. The only sound was the slow deliberate drip of water from a faucet somewhere. It had a warning sound. Cherry and Gwen held their breaths. Up on the dim platform, Miss Sally Chase slept on unsuspectingly.

Cherry and Gwen did not stop to talk. Gwen carefully folded back the covers, while Cherry lifted out the big rubber doll. It swayed a little in her grasp, for it was unmanageably light and bulky.

"Miss Chase seems to have a mind of her own," Cherry panted. "She prefers to stay."

Gwen was hunching up the covers to hide the doll's absence. Cherry, her hands shaking a little, managed to force the floating creature into Ann's housecoat. Her feet, size eleven, had to be folded over to fit into the slippers. Meanwhile Gwen noiselessly rolled over a wheel chair. The two girls worked fast. They sat Sally Chase up in the chair and draped her head and face in the filmy disguising scarf. Then they stood back to admire her.

"Isn't she sweet?" Gwen giggled.

"She's fat but quite good looking," Cherry said, "*and* fairly convincing."

They walked as if on eggs down the length of the classroom, pushing gently, for the doll wobbled as it sat up in the chair. They eased the wheel chair into the nurses' self-service car. They dared not use the regular elevators, and they could only trust to luck that no one would ring for the self-service car on the main floor.

Cherry and Gwen pressed the "Go" button frantically and the automatic door closed—with such a bang that Sally Chase's head fell forward on her knees. They hastily picked her up and barely had set her to rights when the automatic door slid open on the second floor. Trying to look nonchalant, they wheeled Miss Chase out. They were at the corridor of the private pavilion. Here they paused again, breathing hard.

Gwen looked at Cherry goggle-eyed. "You've turned pale for once," she whispered.

Cherry smiled weakly. "In that case, Dr. Wylie should see me now—or should he?"

From the shadow of a doorway, she looked around for Ann, who was posted as guard, spy, and general lookout. She spotted Ann's probationer's gray at the far end of the corridor, near Room One, and had to laugh. Ann looked so dignified and virtuous and busy.

"Hssssst!" Cherry let go cautiously.

Ann turned and instantly her poise vanished. She peered quickly in all directions and with a face full of panic, waved them to come ahead. Cherry and Gwen, stumbling and clutching their huge unwieldy patient, made a wild dash for it. Finally they reached the fatal end door. Ann flung it open, they rounded the wheel chair in, and Ann closed the door noiselessly, remaining outside.

"Whew!" Gwen exclaimed. Her red hair had fallen into her eyes and her hands gripped the chair handle as if welded to it. Cherry was beyond speech. She had one awful thought: "We got it in here all right, but how are we going to get it out again?"

"Hello!" said the child in the bed. Her voice was delighted. "Is that—that big lady in the pretty dress—is she a *doll*?"

"She is," Cherry said, warming to the reason for this whole escapade. "A big doll, bigger than you are. She's come to pay you a visit. She can't stay long, but you can play with her for a while. And on Wednesday I'll get you another doll—one you can keep forever. This one will cheer you up for now. But remember, it's a secret."

"Secret," the child agreed. Her small face was radiant. "I never did see such a wonderful, beautiful doll! So big! Like a real grown-up princess." She beamed ecstatically on the rubber figure. "Is she going to a ball in that lovely dress?"

Gwen advanced to the edge of the bed, pushing the wheel chair into a corner. Her expression was a mixture of sympathy and panic. "Where she's going is a great secret. You mustn't tell anyone she's been here. This is a Mystery Doll."

Cherry swallowed her comment on that.

The little girl nodded. "Is she sick?" she asked gravely. "Like me?"

"She has a rare case of buttonitis," Gwen explained. "She has an awful sweet tooth for buttons and she overate."

The child giggled and turned a fascinated small face to watch Cherry lift the doll out of the wheel chair.

Picking up Sally Chase was like grappling with a zeppelin. A large rubber hand flopped in Cherry's face, to the little girl's amusement. A round shapeless arm bounced across Cherry's shoulder. "She's dancing with you!" the child cried.

"Yes, we're dancing," Cherry gasped, galloping

through a kind of waltz with the doll. "Isn't she graceful?" Cherry panted.

"Isn't she lovely and exquisite! Such clothes! I say, she's awfully big. Do tell me her name!"

"Her name—uh—" Gwen gulped. "That's where the mystery comes in."

Cherry lifted the bouncing, grinning figure onto the bed. The child laid her cheek against its ludicrous face. "But such a beautiful doll must have a name. Nurse, you know what? I'm going to call her Sally."

"No, don't!" both girls exclaimed in horror. Cherry suggested quickly, "Call her Minnie. That suits her personality much better."

The small patient tried to cuddle the enormous doll. She seemed to have many confidential things to whisper to Miss Sally Chase, alias Minnie, now alias Mona. Some of them, from her excited happy whispers, seemed to concern Mummy and London and impossible plans for going home.

For several minutes, Cherry and Gwen listened with their hearts as well as their ears. Cherry had known there was a war raging on the other side of the world, but she had not thought much about it. Now it occurred to her that it was very much her business—her personal business and her business as a nurse-to-be.

She murmured to Gwen, "You know, if we weren't nurses, we'd never have happened to find this little girl."

Gwen replied sturdily, "Well, who else but a nurse happens to be around when people need help?"

Voices outside the door froze them to the spot—the questioning voice of a woman, and Ann's voice, stalling for time. The little girl seemed to notice nothing—surely she would have recognized the voice of her own nurse, if that's who it was. Cherry and Gwen could not hear the words. But they could hear, to their vast relief, Ann sounding as cool and firm as the Superintendent of Nurses herself. Then there was silence.

Presently the door opened a crack. Ann's face, very scared, peeked though. "Floor su—pervisor! Told her doctor—in consultation—in here—she wanted to—know—why—no consultation sign on—door." She wet her lips and added hastily, "You kids better get out of there. Quick."

Cherry and Gwen ran for the cardboard "Do Not Disturb" sign and shoved it through toward Ann. But she backed off from the placard as if it might bite her.

"Suppose," she wailed, "suppose the doctor or the nurse on this case comes along and sees that sign!" Footsteps sounded in the corridor and the door closed abruptly.

"Doctor," the little girl chirped. "I have a doctor. His name is Dr. Wylie."

"What!" Cherry jumped, while Gwen gave a low groan.

"He's terribly nice," the child said. "I like him. He's what my mummy calls a sweet old thing."

"Childhood innocence," Cherry said under her breath. "Gwen, I don't think I care to meet Dr. Wylie in here. Not today. We've got to pack up and start on our travels."

Cherry went over to the bed and gently disengaged Sally Chase from the little English girl's arms, explaining that the doll had to keep an appointment with another doll who was expecting her for supper. Gwen was rapidly readjusting the wheel chair and Cherry was reeling across the room with the doll, when the door flew open. Over Ann's suppressed shriek, a doctor walked in.

Cherry buried her face in Sally's rubber bosom and closed her eyes. There was a loud thump. "That's Gwen fainting," she thought out of the blankness.

"What are you idiots doing?" demanded a horrified masculine voice.

Cherry knew that voice. And it was not Dr. Wylie's. Painfully she opened her eyes. Around Sally Chase's billowing curves, she saw young Dr. James Clayton. He looked positively flabbergasted. Finally he poked Sally with one disbelieving finger.

"She wanted a doll," Cherry whispered weakly. She looked around for Gwen. There was a faint creak from the floor but no Gwen. "There's two of us," Cherry managed to get out at last.

"Two what?"

"Two nice nurses," the little girl said enthusiastically. "They brought me Mona."

"Mona? Who's Mona?"

At that moment Gwen's head rose inch by inch from behind the back of the wheel chair.

"I suppose you're Mona," Dr. Clayton said.

"You don't know anything, do you?" the little girl said pityingly from the bed. Dr. Clayton started. "Mona is the doll. It's a Mystery Doll," the child explained.

Dr. Clayton's humorous young mouth tightened at the corners. "I see no mystery about this. It's only too clear. Would it interest you to know, young ladies, that this child is here on Private Pavilion, instead of Children's Ward or Orthopedic, because she is very nervous and is not supposed to have visitors? Fortunately her wealthy American aunt can afford this. Unfortunately, the aunt had to go away on business and entrusted poor little Pamela here to her private secretary. The secretary apparently isn't too understanding about children." He glanced critically at the toys, then continued hurriedly, "Would it also interest you to know that you could be expelled for this prank and that Dr. Wylie is due here in less than five minutes?"

A faint warning thump on the door corroborated his words. Ann was still sticking to her post.

Dr. Clayton was worried, but he was also trying hard not to laugh. "Tell your guard to get off this pavilion.

And you, Miss Ames, stop hugging that absurd doll."
Gwen ran to the door, and Ann fled. The door closed
again.

"Now then," he said in a low rapid voice. "How did
you get that enormous thing in here?"

They told him. "It's a wonderful new kind of p'ram-
bulator," the little girl contributed.

"Well, we're going to use something safer to get it
back to the classroom," Dr. Jim Clayton said. "If Dr.
Wylie should see you with that—er—curious-looking
creature, you'd never fool him. Or anybody."

He went to the door and called, "Orderly!" Cherry
and Gwen could not hear the brief orders he gave to
the attendant. He turned back into the room. "One of
you probationers is all I'll need. The other one might as
well escape alive."

"I'll stick it out," Cherry said bravely. "After all, it
was my idea."

"Are you sure?" Gwen said sadly. "Well, good-by,
Cherry. Good-by." It sounded like a final farewell. She
swept up Ann's robe and slippers and scarf, slipped
through the half-open door and sprinted out of sight.

Young Dr. Clayton glowered at Cherry. "I came in
here on a social visit—don't know why I'm fool enough
to take a risk like this—but then I got myself in some
messes, too, when I was a student." He smiled suddenly
and Cherry recognized a kindred soft heart.

The orderly brought in a wheeled table, the sort

Cherry had seen on its way back and forth from the operating rooms.

"Thanks, George, and take the wheel chair with you," Dr. Clayton said formally. "I'll handle the table myself." The orderly withdrew, pushing the empty wheel chair.

Cherry and the little girl watched, fascinated. Dr. Clayton lifted the rubber figure onto the table top and covered it with a sheet. "We now have," he said, "a corpse."

"What's a corpse?" asked the child drowsily.

"Tell you tomorrow," Dr. Clayton promised, "if you keep all this a secret. Remember, now."

Dr. Clayton pushed the table out into the hall, Cherry meekly trotting after him. From the third door down issued Dr. Wylie's commanding voice. They did not look up, nor even look at each other. The only other sounds were the swish of their rubber-soled shoes and the wagon's rubber wheels on the linoleum. A nurse approached them, nodded to Dr. Clayton, and passed on. They got onto the elevator safely enough. The operator, and a student nurse on the elevator, looked puzzled when Dr. Clayton said, "Basement, please." But nothing happened.

The basement was deserted. They gained the classroom and groped about in the dark, not daring to turn on the lights. In double-quick time Cherry had restored Sally Chase to her own familiar bed.

She returned to find Dr. Jim Clayton very serious. She saw, in the half-light from the basement, that his face had lost its engaging grin.

"Look here, Cherry Ames," he said. She looked up obediently. "Don't you ever do such a thing again." Cherry dropped her eyes. He went on soberly. "A hospital is an arena where there's a life and death fight going on every minute of the twenty-four hours in a day. A hospital demands the most and the best you have in you to give. It's a place where impossible dreams are made to come true—where every mistake might be fatal and no second chances given—where people's lives are stripped down to the essentials—" He lifted his head and he seemed to be gazing at a vision. Cherry was moved and a little surprised that he should reveal to her how deeply he felt about medicine. Self-doubts stirred uneasily within her.

"And this hospital in particular," he went on. "Well, it's our hospital and I love it," he said simply. "Its traditions are a lot to live up to. Dr. Wylie, whom everybody thinks so harsh, has given forty years of his life to make this a fine hospital. So you see—" He broke off, a little embarrassed.

"Yes, I see," Cherry said, very low. She felt so ashamed of herself she was almost in tears.

After a long minute, Dr. Clayton said, "I think you'll make a fine responsible nurse. A few high jinks never hurt anyone. Just work hard and you'll get there. But don't break any more rules—at least not until you're off probation." There was the merest shadow of a smile on his face.

Cherry looked up at him gratefully. "Thank you for believing in me. I—I'm not sure yet whether I believe in my ability to be a nurse. And thank you for getting us out of a scrape."

"Sure thing. Good night." He turned up the stairs and Cherry was left alone. She stood for a moment in the basement, thinking. She had gotten off easily— more easily than she deserved. What a way for a nurse to behave, even a beginner! From now on, she vowed, she would be less impetuous.

As she crossed the dark lawn to the Nurses' Residence, she mused about Dr. Jim Clayton. "He must like me to take such a chance," she thought, and then instantly reminded herself, "You're here to study, not to daydream. But just the same, he is a darling." In a daze she rode the creaky elevator up to her room, went in and switched on the light.

Stretched out flat in the center of the floor was Gwen. Curled up on the bed was Ann. They were both fast asleep.

CHAPTER VI

The Problem of Vivian Warren

MISS MAC WAS SHOWING THE CLASS HOW TO APPLY HOT wet dressings. They had come a long way in the past month and a half from temperature taking, alcohol sponges and bed baths all the way to giving hypodermics and making solutions, not only in Nursing Arts class but on the wards as well. Cherry thought proudly, as she leafed through her notebook, that she finally had mastered bedmaking and poultices after all.

Miss McIntyre's lively impatient voice brought Cherry's attention back to today's lesson.

"—hot means *hot*, and wet means soaking wet." Miss McIntyre's deft manicured hands applied solution from a rubber syringe onto Sally Chase's imaginary infected wound and covered it with a rubber sheet.

Behind Cherry, Mai Lee's low voice repeated, "Hot . . . wet . . . rubber. . . ." The class was used to

Mai Lee's conscientious echo by now. Over in another corner of the room, Cherry saw plump Bertha Larsen waving her hands in the air, in an abstracted imitation of Miss McIntyre's motions. Behind her sat blonde little Marie Swift, not pampered-looking any longer, scribbling like mad in her notebook. Apart from the rest, with her look of cold contempt, sat Vivian Warren. Cherry wondered fleetingly where Vivian had acquired such an unpleasant disposition and why. She burrowed further into her own chair, warmly conscious of Ann and Gwen on either side of her.

Miss McIntyre stopped for breath, then went on crisply, "Raise the wounded part on a pillow—put hot water bottles outside the rubber—" she did all these quickly as she spoke, "and cover the whole thing, gently please, with a blanket or a piece of flannel. Any questions?"

The only sound was the scratching of pencils on paper as the class raced to keep up, and Mai Lee murmuring, "Pillow, hot water bottles, gently please. . . ." The rubber demonstration doll was the only one in the room who was not hard at work. There were no questions.

"Well, aren't there any questions?" Miss McIntyre demanded. She straightened her cap on her dashing bob. "Do you all know everything there is to know about this?"

Vivian Warren raised her hand confidently. "Is it

correct that this surgical dressing is not necessarily a post-operative technique?"

"Whew!" Gwen whispered into Cherry's ear. "Where did Warren learn all those professional words?"

Ann whispered shrewdly in Cherry's other ear, "She probably memorized that out of the text to impress teacher."

And Miss McIntyre was impressed. "Correct. The wound might be an infected finger, for instance. And very good, Miss Warren."

Vivian settled back in her chair with a satisfied smile. Cherry caught herself wondering whether Vivian could actually do the hot wet dressing. She had made a reputation for herself in Miss McIntyre's class—and through that, in the Training School Office itself—as the outstanding probationer, chiefly by use of her glib tongue. Cherry was considered second best student in her class. But what Vivian's practice on the ward was, nobody knew. Vivian Warren had been quick—a little too quick—to make a personal friend of her supervising head nurse. And Bertha Larsen, who was on ward duty with her, was too loyal to gossip or complain about anyone. Cherry choked over such tactics and so did the rest of the class.

It was especially annoying now, for it was late October, with little more than a month to go until caps. The probationers, constantly being checked these three trial months on performance and personal conduct by T.S.O., were in a state of tension as the time for caps— or expulsion—grew shorter and shorter. Three girls already had dropped out, even before the probationary period was completed. No one knew whether they had lost courage, or whether T.S.O. had asked them to leave. Apparently Vivian Warren was determined to win her cap, no matter what it cost anyone else. But this was no moment to speculate about Vivian's great success by doubtful means, for Miss McIntyre was up and at them with another topic: patient psychology. Although there was a separate class in psychology, the human angle kept cropping up even in classes in technique.

It was Cherry's favorite topic, and visions of Mrs. Brownlee on Women's Medical floated before her as Miss McIntyre, perched jauntily on her desk, talked to them about patient psychology. This time Cherry had a question.

"What do you do with a patient who, though she is nearly well now, is still as cranky and unreasonable as a three-year-old child?"

Before the instructor could answer, Vivian Warren said cuttingly, "A patient reflects his nurse's attitude. A nurse must learn to be calm and unruffled at all times." That, too, was almost word for word out of an earlier lesson.

Cherry was furious. "I *am* calm and unruffled!" she said in excitement and dropped her notebook with a bang.

Vivian Warren raised a skeptical eyebrow. The class looked amused. Cherry could feel her cheeks flushing.

Miss McIntyre said sharply, "Please let us have no quarreling in class."

To Cherry's surprise, Josie Franklin spoke up in her defense. "This patient is really unusually difficult."

But Josie's apologetic tone only made matters worse. "Doesn't Miss Ames know that that's where the nurse's skill comes in?" asked Vivian Warren innocently.

Miss McIntyre said even more sharply than before, "That will do, Miss Warren!"

Cherry had a dozen hot-tempered answers on the tip of her tongue and Gwen's red head was stuck out like a danger signal. But Miss McIntyre was going on with the lecture.

Cherry left the classroom at the end of the period, sputtering with indignation. Vivian Warren was doing her best to spread the impression that Cherry could not handle her patients. And it was not true!

Gwen whispered furiously, "I'm just sorry that murder isn't legal!"

Ann was angry, too, in her quiet controlled way. "Cherry's too good a student. Vivian's afraid."

"She's a mean deceitful perfectly nasty person," Josie said all in one breath. She had come up behind them in the hall, and they all walked along together to laboratory practice.

Cherry said nothing. She was thinking of what Ann had said. The clue repeated itself over and over, "Vivian's afraid, Vivian's afraid . . . afraid . . . afraid . . ." Just when they entered the laboratory, a wisp of an idea formed in her mind. She said nothing to the girls but merely went to her stool at the long sink and slipped on her white coat.

The idea swelled and grew, as Cherry bent and applied one dark eye to the bacteria slide under her microscope. She loved the big gray steel-and-stone laboratory, with its complete set of equipment for each student, and she loved uncovering the mysteries of living things under the delicate and powerful microscope. The wet solution on her hands, the sound of running water, the deep voice of the instructor in the next aisle, even the strong smell of formaldehyde, were familiar and pleasant. How Dr. Joe would enjoy working with all these fine instruments—and what good use he could put them to! "I must write him again about his new drug," Cherry reminded herself. But even Dr. Joe was blotted out by Ann's phrase, "Vivian's afraid . . . afraid . . ." What was she afraid of? Cherry had some ideas of her own about that.

She polled Ann and Gwen on their way to nutrition class.

"La Warren is afraid of failing," was Gwen's guess.

"And if she can't succeed by fair means, then she'll succeed by foul."

"But we're all worried about probation," Ann pointed out. "Or are you two relatives of Richard the Lion-Hearted? No, Miss Jones, I'd say that Warren knows she isn't any too competent and is trying hard to cover up."

"Yes, you're both right, but," Cherry said slowly, "there's something else besides. She's so gosh-awful desperate about not failing——"

"A desperate character?" Gwen giggled. They saw Vivian walking ahead of them. She was alone, as always. Certainly her poised manner did not suggest desperation.

"Yes, she *is* taking this awfully hard," Cherry insisted. "We all have our hearts set on being nurses. But she acts as if failure would be a death sentence. She's willing to do *anything* to win her cap, as if—as if, should she get tossed out of here, she wouldn't dare go back to where she came from."

The three girls looked at one another. "Where *did* she come from?" Ann asked. They did not know. Vivian Warren had not told anyone anything about herself.

The idea in back of Cherry's bright black eyes was becoming clearer now. She entered the dietetic laboratory feeling a bit like a detective, but still she said nothing.

Dietetics was always fun. Last time the class had had a lecture on nutrition, with emphasis on bland diets, so today each girl was at her own stove making those vitamins taste good. Cherry enjoyed having a stove, sink, and shining utensils all to herself. "It's like playing house," she thought, as she stirred the cream soup and took a quick worried look at the junket. Cherry noticed, with a twinkle, that Bertha was taking more tastes of her cooking than strictly necessary. Well, this class did make one hungry. "Here's hoping my cooking will smell as tantalizing to a sick person as it does to me," Cherry thought, her mouth watering. Even Vivian Warren thawed out in dietetics lab, her rather hard face carefully studying the contents of the pan which quiet little Mai Lee obligingly held out to her. "Afraid . . . afraid . . ." went the ticking in Cherry's head.

The nutrition instructor, Mrs. Gaynor, a plump motherly woman, wandered from one stove to another, sniffing, tasting, poking spoons into pots and explaining as she went. "Don't forget, girls," she called out, "it has to *look* nice, too. Many patients never want to hear of food again, so you have to tempt them with *eye* appeal. *Small* portions, girls, they can always have seconds . . ." Over Cherry's shoulder, Mrs. Gaynor said, "Smooth and creamy, Miss Ames, that's it. You have the knack." Cherry was pleased. She glanced up just in time to see Vivian Warren frown. But the idea was almost whole now and Cherry felt confident. Mrs. Gaynor's voice went on at the next stove, "No, my dear. Stir, *stir!* How would *you* like LUMPS?"

Lumps or no lumps, the class moved on to anatomy lesson. This was a stiff course. Even Dr. Jim Clayton had admitted to Cherry, one day on the ward, that he would need to brush up on anatomy and physiology before he could keep up with her studies. Cherry was not too happy amid the bones and the diagrams of nerves and arteries. But all this certainly did explain what treatments were required for her patients on Women's Medical with such illnesses as cardiac disorder, rheumatic fever, and ulcers. Not even Vivian Warren dared speak up here, and it was a chastened class that streamed downstairs to the nurses' pleasant green dining room.

Cherry was suspiciously quiet at lunch. She and Ann and Gwen shared the sunny corner table with Josie, Bertha, blonde little Marie Swift and Mai Lee.

Gwen was imitating Mrs. Gaynor's pouter pigeon bosom and exhorting the others, "*Plenty* of milk, girls, just plunk it in your junket! How would *you* like toast like a leather sole? Now, girrrrls——"

Cherry smiled absent-mindedly at the banter, but she was watching for something. There was a chair vacant at their table. There were vacant chairs, too, with other members of the probationers' class. Vivian Warren came by with a laden tray from the food counter and sat down with a group of more advanced student nurses. Why? They did not seem to know her and Vivian was as alone with her salad as if she were an isolated measles case. Now that she thought of it, Cherry had always seen Vivian alone. But only now had she taken the time to think it over.

"Look at Cherry nodding to herself!" Ann said. "We'll take her over to Psychiatric right after lunch."

"All right, but I'll miss you, all of you," Cherry assured them.

"Maybe we'll go crazy and come to see you," Gwen said with her tongue in her cheek. "Come on, confess."

Marie Swift wrinkled up her nose. "I smell a mystery."

"Ames has a plan about Warren," Ann guessed.

But Cherry appeared absolutely fascinated with her vegetables. By the time they had finished their pudding —and they had a strong suspicion that it was their own junket lurking under the chocolate sauce—Cherry still had not recovered from her deliberate attack of deafness to their questions. The idea was in full bloom now. But first there was ward duty to be completed.

Toiling up the stairs to the ward, Josie Franklin said, "You're in a real sweet temper, considering how that Warren behaved in class this morning."

"Mmm," said Cherry, and glanced quickly at Josie. But Josie's candid face was innocent of subterfuge.

Cherry paused at Miss Baker's desk to say "Good

afternoon" and report on duty. The pretty head nurse smiled up at her. "If Miss McIntyre has taught you how to make soap solution, you are just the person Ward 4 needs."

"Let Ward 4 rejoice," Cherry said and Miss Baker grinned back at her. Inwardly Cherry was rejoicing that Miss Baker thought her capable enough to do this job. Marjory Baker was a darling, anyway, Cherry thought. She was sorry her month on Women's Medical was nearly up, for she would have to be transferred to another ward where she would sample another branch of nursing.

By now Ward 4 was practically home. It was a good feeling to walk down the long row of white beds, smiling hello to the patients, who looked up eagerly from their lunch trays to smile back. Even grumpy Mrs. Brownlee. Even the three new patients who had been admitted last week, and the new young woman who had been brought in yesterday and occupied the little Southerner's bed. It gave Cherry a good satisfying feeling, and her cheeks were very pink and her black curls bounced. Now she really understood Mrs. Brownlee's diabetic condition and the Slavic woman's cardiac case and the case of the girl who had mistakenly swallowed poison. Best of all, Cherry thought, as she trotted toward the kitchen to help serve the lunch trays, was knowing what she, Cherry Ames, could do to help them. Cherry could not help wondering if the star student, Vivian Warren, felt the same or did as well on the ward.

In the small steamy kitchen, Miss Antonio and Miss Prentice were arranging trays at top speed and calling each other good-humored names. Josie, not altogether sure they were joking, huddled in a corner preparing trays of house diets.

"Want a hand?" Cherry offered.

"Come on in," Miss Prentice said. She had thawed out considerably in the past month. "Always room for one more."

Cherry squeezed in and reached for the trays.

"Have you heard?" Miss Antonio said over the clatter of dishes. "Mrs. Thompson—" that was the granite-faced woman who disapproved of all nurses under forty, "—is being discharged today. I took her final check-up this morning. And you know what that means."

Cherry disengaged herself from thoughts of the Vivian Warren campaign.

Josie asked trustingly, "What does that mean?"

"It means, my innocent little lamb," Miss Antonio replied, "that the whole ward will want to go home too. They're all so nearly well, they are getting restless. Wish we could just spirit Mrs. Thompson out of here in the middle of the night. As it is—" she sighed.

Later as Cherry collected trays and adjusted pillows, there was a buzz of excitement on the ward. Voices called from bed to bed. No one wanted to settle down for the afternoon nap. The most stubborn one of all, and the only silent woman on the ward, was Mrs. Thompson. She sat grimly propped against her pillow, her two braids of gray hair like guns over her shoulders.

"I'll wait for Dr. Clayton," was all she would say, even to Miss Baker. So the entire ward waited for the young interne.

Cherry went off to make soap solution and when she returned, Dr. Clayton was at Mrs. Thompson's bedside. Cherry felt a surge of pleasure at seeing him and thought again what vitality and hope this tall young doctor brought into the ward. Just now, however, there was an argument going on.

"But, Mrs. Thompson, you are quite well enough to go home," Dr. Clayton was saying. "See here, your chart shows——"

"I'm not leaving," Mrs. Thompson said flatly.

Miss Baker came to Dr. Clayton's side. "We need your bed and your nurses for other sick people. You know how shorthanded we are, with doctors and nurses going off to the battle fronts. Surely you know what a serious shortage civilian hospitals like ours are up against. There are sick people waiting and we have no nurses to take care of them."

Mrs. Thompson compressed her lips so tightly they looked like a ruled line. "I refuse to leave the hospital."

Dr. Clayton said wearily, "But why?" The whole ward was listening.

"I like it here. The doctors and the nurses are all so nice, and the meals are good, and everything's done for me. Why it's the first time in my life I ever had a vacation. It's a real pleasure to be sick in a good hospital. No, sirree, I'm staying right here."

Cherry smothered an impulse to laugh. Mrs. Thompson had "hospitalitis!" What could Dr. Clayton or the head nurse say to that? Jim Clayton and Marjory Baker sought each other's eyes in despair.

"We're glad we've succeeded in keeping you comfortable and happy," Miss Baker said tactfully. "We feel that's half the reason why you've made such a good recovery. But don't you want to return to your own house and see how your family is?"

The stony-faced woman showed her first glimmer of feeling. She hesitated, then said, "Oh, they're all right. I'd just as soon never go back."

Never go back! Something clicked in her mind.

To Cherry's surprise, her feet carried her forward, without her permission, and her voice was speaking of its own accord. Cherry heard herself saying, "What about that daughter of yours who hasn't the sense of a chicken? The young one like me, I mean? I'll bet she's neglected to oil the furniture and chipped all the dishes and scorched the linens by now." The woman's face changed. "She's probably let your garden run to weed too. Of course I don't want to worry you, Mrs. Thompson, but I'd be surprised if that daughter of yours hasn't forgotten to air the mattresses—and she's probably opened all your best jams and jellies too!"

The patient's face was by now thoroughly alarmed. Cherry had found what was closest to her heart. She threw back the blanket with one sweep of her bony arm and commanded, "Put up a screen around my bed! My best pillow slips ruined, I don't doubt, and nothing left of the good Damson plum I slaved over last year . . . I'm getting dressed!" She went on talking excitedly as Cherry brought the white cotton shirred screen and then slipped away.

The whole ward was convulsed with laughter, but Miss Baker stood in the middle of the aisle with her finger pressed warningly against her lips. Blankets heaved under silently shaking shoulders. Dr. Jim Clayton was so amused that he had to leave in haste. In the general though smothered mirth, Miss Antonio hustled Mrs. Thompson out before the rest of the ward had time to fret about not being discharged too.

The moment her angry, anxious footsteps had died away down the corridor, the ward rang with laughter.

"Oh, Miss Ames," Miss Baker gulped when she could get her breath, "you were wonderful. Inspired."

"I just hope—" Cherry said, and broke off. What she hoped was that she would be as successful with Vivian Warren as with Mrs. Thompson. Vivian was younger and tougher and might turn out to be more than Cherry could cope with.

By the time Cherry had given her share of the patients their evening care, and settled them for supper and the night, it was four-thirty. She reported off duty to Miss Baker and looked around for Josie. She found her changing water for the flowers.

"Don't wait for me," Josie said. "I'll be another ten minutes in this hothouse."

Cherry went off alone. It was just as well she was alone, she thought, with what she planned to do.

Not that she liked what she had to do. But she was going to have trouble with Vivian Warren sooner or later. Better to nip it in the bud right now. Cherry also remembered something out of her brother's military manual about the value of a "surprise attack." She did not mean to attack unless Vivian made that necessary. She intended something quite different. But in any event, Vivian was going to be surprised.

Cherry slipped across the lobby of Spencer, avoiding the library and the lounge. She walked across the lawn to the Nurses' Residence, entered the creaky elevator, and got off on the floor below her own. Two girls from her section passed her in the corridor, but Cherry only smiled and did not stop to talk. The ideas she had been considering in topsy-turvy order all this busy day arranged themselves in a plan now. Afraid—perhaps Vivian would be more afraid of this interview than Cherry. And those bullying tactics of Vivian's—the sure sign of a coward, of someone afraid. If only she could put her finger on the cause of that fear. Cherry stopped before Vivian Warren's room and knocked.

There was a faint rustle within, then silence. Cherry rapped again. The door opened and Vivian Warren stood there, looking astonished.

"May I come in?" Cherry's voice was pleasant, but there was a ring of challenge in it.

"If you like," Vivian said coldly, and Cherry entered. The room was like all the others, except that Vivian had none of the little personal knickknacks the other girls treasured. Cherry sat down on a chair. Vivian seated herself stiffly on the bed and waited.

"You probably know without my telling you," Cherry started, "that I think your tactics against me in class are pretty unfair. I want to tell you very plainly that I don't like them."

She watched the other girl closely, measuring the effect of her words. Not a muscle in that guarded face moved. If Cherry had expected a bold reply, none was forthcoming. Vivian's eyes glinted, but she said nothing. Cherry went on quietly but firmly:

"I also want to tell you that I won't stand for that sort of thing. You'll have to stop it or—" she gambled on Vivian's basic cowardice "—you are going to find yourself in trouble."

Vivian Warren dropped her eyes. Cherry waited. But Vivian did not have the courage to fight in the open. Cherry felt relieved. She had already half won. She much preferred to have no fight at all.

"But that isn't what I came to say," Cherry went on.

Vivian looked up curiously. "It isn't? What else is there?"

"You. I don't know you. Nobody knows you. I can't help wondering why you feel you have to resort to such tactics, when you're every bit as capable as the next student, and why you're always alone."

Vivian twisted her hands together and was silent for a moment. "Do you know," she said, "you're the first person who's ever come to my room to see me? There hasn't been another soul."

She glanced up furtively again and for the first time Cherry could see into the other girl's eyes. What she saw was loneliness and fear.

They talked for a long time, slowly and painfully at first. Then Vivian's words came pouring out in an emotional storm as she admitted her need to tell someone. Vivian's bravado was gone now, and Cherry gradually learned a story that amazed her. Vivian came from a desperately poor and wretched family. Her father had been a drunkard for years. Her mother had long since given up hope and ambition for her many children. Home meant nothing to Vivian but squalor and fights. At school she had been despised as a member of "that awful Warren family." She had grown up believing that she was not as good or as bright as the other young people and that she had better distrust everyone and look out for herself by any means possible. She was embittered and hard. Nursing stood for something clean and decent and orderly to her, and it meant having a home for the first time in her life. She had worked for two years in a laundry to save up enough to enter the nursing school. Now she was counting on winning a government scholarship from the U. S. Cadet Corps to get through.

"I have to make good here, I have to!" Vivian cried to Cherry. "If I don't, I have no place else to go—I haven't a cent—I'm all alone— And I can't go home, I can't, I won't!" She shuddered, and for a moment Cherry thought she was going to weep. She added sternly, "Not even T.S.O. knows this. I'm ashamed. I don't want anyone to know."

Cherry listened to all this, feeling stirred and deeply sorry. She tried to imagine herself in Vivian's place, tried to feel as Vivian felt, but she could not. Her own life had been so happy and normal. She only knew that if Vivian's fears could be banished, there was a nice girl waiting to be coaxed out from under that hard shell. Cherry took a deep breath.

"See here, Vivian," she said. "All that's behind you now. And you don't have to go on hating and distrusting people. People will be nice to you if you only let them. You'll make good here, and on merit alone. See how well you've done already! And honestly you don't have to treat us all as enemies. We want to like you. We want you to like us."

Vivian looked at her through narrowed eyes. Cherry thought of a hunted animal. "I don't believe you," Vivian Warren said coldly.

Cherry sighed. She knew that it would take a long time to overcome the fears Vivian had grown up with. So she said only, "We're all going to the movies after dinner. Come along. We can get back safely before ten."

Vivian rose and held the door open. "You don't really want me. And the other girls don't. I'm not fooled."

Cherry rose too. "We're meeting in the lobby at seven. Wear your hat and coat. It's getting cold out these fall nights." Vivian did not reply. Her face was sullen.

Cherry turned to say one more thing before she left. "I'm glad I'm getting to know you. And I hope you'll return my visit."

Only her footsteps broke the strained silence as she walked down the hall.

At dinner Cherry did not see Vivian Warren anywhere in the dining room, and that troubled her. She could not take part in the conversation around her.

"Very sad about Ames," Gwen said, shaking her red head. "Did you hear? I wish she were here, the poor girl, I'd try to help her."

Ann's dark blue eyes crinkled in a smile. "She's obviously not here."

Cherry said feebly, "Present," and relapsed into her thoughts. When the other probies were discussing, over their coffee, the movie they were to see, Cherry roused herself long enough to remark:

"I've asked some of the other girls to come along."

"Fine," Ann agreed.

"Sure, the more the merrier," Gwen said. "Come on, let's collect ourselves—Josie, Mai Lee, Marie, Bertha —" Four other classmates trooped along, too. Second dinner had begun and still Vivian Warren had not appeared. At seven they slipped into their coats and went out to the lobby to meet the rest of the theater party. Cherry glanced around the lobby, holding her breath.

Standing alone by the elevator, clutching her coat and looking both afraid and eager, was Vivian Warren. Her eyes were red about the rims.

Cherry smiled and waved, and was rewarded by a faint smile forming with difficulty on the other girl's lips. Vivian came toward them with uncertain steps, like a person just learning to walk.

"Our star probationer is not above movies!" Cherry

announced gaily. And the other girls, taking Cherry's cue, welcomed Vivian cordially into the group.

"I've won!" Cherry thought as she went down the steps with Vivian by her side. "I've won!" And it was a double victory—one for herself and one for Vivian Warren.

CHAPTER VII

Ames's Folly

CHERRY'S OLD ENEMY TIME HAD CAUGHT UP WITH her. She was leaving Ward 4. Cherry was sorry to say good-by to Miss Baker, who understood a probationer's sorrows, and the familiar patients who had practically adopted her. She was sorry, too, to part from Josie Franklin who was also going to wards unknown. But say good-by she must, for it was November, the fateful third month of probation was starting, and she was being transferred to Ward 27.

"Never mind," Miss Baker consoled her as they stood in the doorway of the old ward. "You can always come back and visit. And we'll want to see how your cap looks on you."

"Wish I were getting my cap on your ward," Cherry said, "if I do get it. What is Ward 27?"

"Men's Surgical. It'll be extremely good experience for you."

"Surgical!" Cherry exclaimed in horror-struck tones. "Dr. Wylie! Don't tell me I'll have to earn my cap on Dr. Wylie's ward!"

At first it seemed to Cherry that everything was for the worst in the worst of all possible wards. Miss Craig, the head nurse, was an old-school disciplinarian, more of a machine than a human being. She was a short, stout, elderly woman with a rigid posture, a voice and temper that crackled like her apron, and a withered smile that seemed mechanical.

As for the three graduate nurses here, they were marvels of efficiency and a little tired of nearly helpless probationers. Cherry suspected that her predecessors, whoever they were, must have made some trying blunders. Cherry found it simpler to keep out of the other nurses' way. Perhaps on another ward, working under a pleasanter head nurse, they might be pleasanter themselves, Cherry realized.

The patients provided another problem. Most of them were very sick, and the others seemed to have caught an unusually gloomy mood. Of course the orderlies did all the necessary bathing and lifting. To be fair, Cherry admitted, the men were much less fussy than women patients, and she could not blame them for not being cheerful. There was nothing cheerful about a ruptured gall bladder or a brain concussion—and all surgeries were serious business.

There were no flowers here, no pastel bed jackets and

laughter of people who were almost well—just masculine silence and a grim routine under Miss Craig's icy eye, and under Dr. Wylie's rigid ruling. He came faithfully every day, sweeping past Cherry, to her relief. In his terrifying way, he forced even the most desperately ill of these men toward recovery.

And it rained. It rained and rained and rained, till Cherry wondered why the ward did not float. "If anyone thinks nursing is romantic," Cherry thought at the end of her first week here, "let him step right this way to Ward 27, please."

But there were two bright spots. Miss Craig was a top-flight nurse and Dr. Wylie was a top-ranking surgeon, and here was Cherry working right alongside the most superb medical talent in the country. The other bright spot was Ann Evans. She had been assigned with Cherry as the ward's other probationer.

"If it weren't for you, you anchor," Cherry told Ann late one afternoon in the kitchen, as they—quite against the rules—sampled bread and butter, "I'd have washed out by now from sheer fright. Why do we have to earn our caps *here* of all places? The toughest surgeon in the hospital!" Cherry sighed as she set to work on the supper trays. "I never was lucky. Never won dolls at the fair, never won at bingo, couldn't even win a booby prize at a party."

Ann said with her mouth full of prunes, "It's not a question of luck. It's merit that counts here. Of course

Dr. Wylie is demanding and that's to his credit—he'll have only the best care for his patients. You must admit, Cherry, that he's absolutely right." Ann carefully swallowed the prunes and started out with the first tray.

"T'ain't luck, no, Ma'am."

"If a little luck came along," Cherry called after her, "I wouldn't turn it down. Not with caps less than a month away."

"Good luck or bad luck?" Ann smiled back as she disappeared into the ward. Cherry was a little startled by that remark. Ann had a way of tossing off the most penetrating insights without warning.

Bad luck was what it turned out to be. During the first two weeks that Cherry and Ann were on Men's Surgical, Dr. Wylie had ignored the probationers. He had seen them all right; he saw everything. Sometimes he came in alone, or sometimes he brought two or three eminent visiting doctors to see some special surgery. Occasionally he entered followed by a group of nervous, respectful internes, whom he lectured as if contemptuous of their ability ever to learn.

On the Thursday afternoon later known as Ames's Folly, Dr. Wylie brought four house doctors with him, among them young Dr. Clayton. It was raining: a cold, unrelenting, late November rain that had been beating monotonously against the windows for three days without let-up. Everyone was edgy. The electric lights were on, giving their faces a yellow look. Even Dr. Wylie looked more razor-sharp than usual as he marched down the row of beds with the tall young internes behind him.

Cherry promptly headed for the linen closet. She could be just as useful among the sheets as making some terrible blunder before Dr. Wylie, she told herself, not to mention Miss Craig and the assembled internes—especially a certain engaging one. Perhaps she looked a little too eager to get away. Dr. Wylie called after her.

"You!" he said in an accusing voice. Everyone froze, even the head nurse. Cherry could feel her heart beating as the steely gray eyes fastened unmistakably upon her. "You will kindly come back here and assist me in changing a dressing."

Cherry walked back slowly, in the manner of a doomed man. Everyone knew that doctors never wanted probationers when there were experienced nurses around. Something was up. Cherry vaguely saw Miss Craig's disapproving face, Ann's blue eyes opened to the size of saucers, and Jim Clayton looking at her sympathetically, as if he were trying to whisper, "Buck up, *I know* you'll do all right." She finally reached Dr. Wylie's side and could smell the strong chemicals which clung to his long white coat. He turned his back to her while he explained the details of the abdominal surgery to the internes.

Cherry listened in fascination to Dr. Wylie. She had

known a little about the case, enough to keep elderly
Mr. Mills on his strict diet and to watch his bandage
carefully for staining. But now here was the whole
story, and it was exciting. Cherry was amused to see
Mr. Mills's proud satisfied glance when his incision
was displayed, as if it were the only case of its kind in
the world. Actually Dr. Wylie was selecting for his
students the most common and typical example of a
complex appendectomy.

Cherry was so interested that when Dr. Wylie said
absently over his shoulder, "Sterile field!" Cherry had
no sterile field ready. She simply stood there, appalled.

Dr. Wylie turned full around. "Sterile instruments!"
he barked. "Why haven't you got them ready?"

Cherry said, "Yes, sir!" and ran. Luckily Ann, out in
the laboratory, had hastily checked the contents of the
dressing carriage. Cherry hurried back pushing the carriage, placed the sterile sheet on Mr. Mills's bed, and
laid sterile instruments and bandages on the sterile field.
Dr. Wylie was fuming. His eyes darted critically from
one object to another—sterile gauze, forceps, one pair
of them in phenol solution, adhesive—fortunately it
was all there. Ann had seen to that, bless her!

"Well? Well?" Dr. Wylie demanded. His eyes went
through her like knives. Cherry became so rattled that
she could not remember what to do next, although she
knew all of it by heart. The older nurses, behind Dr.
Wylie's back, were frantically going through motions of

washing their hands and one of them quickly trundled a screen around Mr. Mills's bed.

Her hands thoroughly scrubbed, Cherry picked up the sterile forceps. A dozen pairs of eyes, huddled inside the screen, watched her lift off the old bandage. At that very moment, she remembered she should have used the phenol forceps instead. The silence was so complete and horrified that the rain on the windows sounded like drums. Funeral drums.

Dr. Wylie snorted. Instantly the head nurse stepped forward. "I'll get you another nurse, sir."

"No!" Dr. Wylie exploded. "This girl's going to learn!"

Cherry hesitated, holding the soiled and infectious bandage in mid-air. And then she dropped it on the bed, just missing the surgeon's immaculate hand. It made a spreading red stain on the clean blanket.

Dr. Wylie opened his mouth in fury but checked himself. Somehow his silence, and his face mottled with anger, were worse than anything he could have said. The head nurse whirled upon her. Cherry was close to tears.

All those internes' faces! Were they laughing at her or suffering along with her? Just as her hand reached out for the phenol forceps, Dr. Wylie grated in her ear, "You in Miss McIntyre's class?"

Cherry jumped and gulped, "Yes, sir," while her hands went on blindly about their business.

There was a gasp from Jim Clayton. She had picked up the wrong forceps again. She had made exactly the same mistake all over again!

The surgeon's narrowed eyes, on a level with Cherry's own, were merciless. "This is inexcusable! Even a student should know an elementary procedure like this!"

"I'm sorry, sir," Cherry managed to stammer.

"Yes, you'd be sorry if the infection spread to other patients—" he bit out "—or if the wound became unclean—then you'd be sorry and a lot of help that would be to the patients! Carelessness!" He set his teeth in his impatience, threw aside the screen and ordered the head nurse to tend to Mr. Mills's dressing.

Cherry dug her hands into her pockets and clenched her fists hard to keep herself under control. She was shaken and humiliated. Behind her there came a buzz of low masculine voices. The internes apparently were discussing her. She could see Jim Clayton's troubled brown eyes.

Miss Craig came up behind her. "It's four-thirty, Miss Ames. You may sign off duty now. We won't be needing you any more this afternoon." Cherry was sure she did not merely imagine the sarcasm.

Cherry reported off with a heavy heart. She looked about for Ann, but the head nurse kept Ann a while longer. Out in the empty corridor Cherry leaned against the wall. She thought bleakly, "There goes my cap."

Dr. Wylie probably would report her to Training School Office. If he did not, that martinet head nurse would. Cherry wandered down the hall, letting her feet carry her where they would. She found herself, somehow, in Ward 4, standing before Miss Baker's desk, looking down into Miss Baker's sympathetic horror-struck face, and telling her what had happened.

Miss Baker was quiet when Cherry had finished. Then she led her out to the corridor, after nodding to the student head nurse to take over.

"You poor little probie," she said. "Of course, you did do wrong, but what beginner wouldn't with Dr. Wylie watching every move? But, after all, a nurse of all people has to keep her head."

"But he needn't have bawled me out so—so cruelly!" Cherry wailed. At Miss Baker's first kind word, she had started to feel sorry for herself.

"Now look here, Cherry Ames," Miss Baker said. "If you were a surgeon with forty years' practice behind you, and you were worried about your patient, you might be pretty annoyed at a blundering probationer yourself!"

Cherry's black eyes grew heavy. Even Miss Baker was going back on her! Cherry knew she was at fault but she was going through a painful ordeal all the same. And just before caps! Her confidence in her ability to be a nurse, her dream of belonging to this profession, seemed to be breaking into bits.

She glanced up out of her misery to see the student head nurse beckoning to Miss Baker. Miss Baker pressed Cherry's hand and hurried off.

"Well, you've had quite an afternoon of it!" said Jim Clayton's voice beside her. Cherry looked up self-consciously at the young doctor. He was not joking, nor teasing her. The sensitive lines of his mouth showed that he appreciated what a torment this was for her.

"I'll never get my cap now," Cherry said dully. "Dr. Wylie and Miss Craig will see to that."

"I think you will," Dr. Clayton said. "I don't believe that either Dr. Wylie or Miss Craig will report you. They're not so bad. And they saw how nervous you were. After you left, Cherry, Dr. Wylie said, 'This rain's getting on everybody's nerves.'" Jim Clayton chuckled. "For him, that's practically a pardon and an apology."

"Then there's still a chance!" Cherry breathed. She noted that this was the first time Jim Clayton had ever called her by her first name.

"And another thing." He put his hand lightly on her shoulder. "Don't let this shake your self-confidence. I know you're going to make a good nurse. I can see it in you. If Dr. Wylie ever upsets you like this again, say to yourself, 'Jim Clayton has confidence in me.'"

Cherry looked up at him with shining eyes. He understood. And he believed in her. She was touched. How did he know how lost and hopeless she felt? As she stood watching him go into Ward 4, she thought, "He does like me! He likes me a great deal. Perhaps it's more than liking, too." And with herself, it could easily be more than liking. His hand on her shoulder, even remembered, made Cherry's heart beat foolishly faster.

But she had little hope of mercy from Dr. Wylie or Miss Craig, despite what Jim Clayton had said. That was just his effort to console her. To Cherry, those two seemed the coldest and sternest mortals she had ever met.

The two final weeks before caps were one long worry for Cherry. All the probationers grew tense. Josie Franklin's nervousness was, for once, not a laughing matter. Bertha becomingly lost weight. Both Vivian Warren and Mai Lee skipped lunch in order to study. Even Gwen did not joke as much as usual. Cherry kept a sharp grip on herself, in her classes and on Men's Surgical. She did not make any further mistakes, partly because Miss Craig coldly took pains to teach her, and partly because the only further remark Dr. Wylie addressed to her was "Humph!"

Examinations came along. Classes went on just the same. Cherry had studied hard for the tests, but then, they counted less than one's general work and character. She knew all her other work to date had been conscientious. She had done the best she could. Or had she? Maybe she had skidded along because Cherry Ames always did pretty well without trying. Dr. Joe had said to her once, "It's too bad things come so easily for you, Cherry—you believe you don't have to make an effort." Now in the last, cold, snowing days before caps, when the probationers went about the hospital with wild looks on their faces and odd replies on their tongues, Cherry thought back to things she had skipped over: charting, for one thing, bed baths, for another. But now it was too late.

There was another, deeper worry: Had Dr. Wylie or, more likely, Miss Craig reported her? There had been no word from T.S.O. But that proved nothing. All she could do was wait.

The day for caps dawned with a little weak sunshine but it rained again and snowed a little before noon. Inside the hospital it was warm and busy and friendly, a whole world at work. The older nurses and the internes were gaily planning the forthcoming Fall Term dance, to mark the end of the first three-month term. The probationers were too wretched to talk about the dance, or about anything. Some of them might not be here for the dance, no longer a part of this bustling hospital. No more joking in the tiny kitchens, nor the good sharp smells of medicines and disinfectants, no more familiar maze of corridors and rows of white beds, no more being needed. Cherry realized for the first time, on this final day, how deeply she had grown into the hospital.

By eleven o'clock word got around among the probationers that Vivian Warren had received her cap—the first probationer to be capped. There were some caustic comments, but Cherry knew all it meant to Vivian and was glad for her. Ann received her cap next, Cherry heard, and rejoiced. By noon Gwen wore the prized cap on her red hair, and a dozen other girls had theirs. Cherry hid her own uneasiness. It was embarrassing at lunch, with some heads self-consciously bearing the foolish, treasured mite of organdie, and other heads still humbly bare.

Out of the noise of congratulations in the dining room, Ann said casually, "They're not giving the caps out in any particular order—not grades or merit or alphabetically or anything."

"That's for me," Cherry thought. She hid her face in her glass as she remembered that, if her old standing of second best in the class still held, she would have had her cap by now. The other probies—and these brand-new, full-fledged student nurses—must be wondering about her. She felt immeasurably lonely. Well, it was her own fault. She should have changed that dressing correctly, no matter how jittery Dr. Wylie made her. She caught Ann's and Gwen's reassuring smiles but nothing helped.

It was even more difficult on the ward. Ann, trying not to look proud, but blushing under her "cream puff," was pressed with congratulations from old Miss Craig and the nurses and the patients, and was stopped in the hall by understanding nurses and internes whom she did not even know. Beside her, Cherry felt that her black curls must be conspicuous. As she went about her work, everyone was painfully careful to be kind and not mention caps to Cherry. As if she were thinking of anything else! Once she caught Miss Craig looking at her thoughtfully.

Two o'clock came and went . . . Josie and Mai Lee got theirs, Ann told her . . . three o'clock . . . three-thirty. And still Cherry was not called. She found it harder and harder to meet Ann's grave eyes. She heard from a maid that two girls in the other section had left, crying. Everyone must be saying by now that Cherry Ames would be dropped, too. When Mr. Mills called out cheerfully, "Hey, Miss Ames, where's yours?" she pretended not to hear and fled.

Three forty-five. Four. Ann tactfully avoided her. Four-fifteen. Four-twenty. Cherry knew now that she would not receive her cap. Dr. Wylie or Miss Craig had reported her after all. Tonight she would be packing, leaving her own little room, leaving the ward and Miss Mac's class, and Ann and Gwen, and all the great hospital world. She worked blindly through the last few, terrible minutes. All she longed for now was to get off the ward and away from the anxious, sympathetic silence of the nurses around her.

At four twenty-five Cherry saw Dr. Jim Clayton come

in and speak briefly to Miss Craig. He left at once. She saw Miss Craig go to the ward phone and heard her call T.S.O. She could not hear the rest of the conversation, and she did not want to. She could guess what this meant: Miss Craig was probably asking T.S.O. to send her another probationer tomorrow to take Cherry's place. Cherry saw Miss Craig hang up, as if watching her in a movie.

"Miss Ames!" the elderly head nurse called. Cherry walked numbly to her desk. "You are to report to Training School Office immediately." She smiled and Cherry wondered what reason there was left even for that automatic smile.

Downstairs in the office, Cherry was surprised when the Superintendent of Nurses herself came out of the inner office with a distracted expression on her usually dignified face.

"Miss Ames, where is your cap?"

Cherry felt the hot tears starting to her eyes as she had to say the bitter words: "I have not received my cap, Miss Reamer."

Miss Reamer frowned and bit her lip. "Will you come in here? I feel very badly that this has happened."

"I feel badly myself," Cherry said very low. "I had wanted so much to be a nurse and now—to fail—perhaps I didn't try hard enough——"

"But after all, Miss Ames, you didn't— Oh, I am so

sorry this had to happen!" Miss Reamer drew Cherry in and closed the door to her office. Four observant pairs of eyes were mercifully shut out. Miss Reamer came over to Cherry and smiled at her warmly.

"My dear child, you haven't failed! There's been an unforgivable slip-up somewhere. If we had a capping ceremony, as some other schools do, this could never have happened. Indeed you haven't failed! You stand second highest in the entire class!"

Cherry was shaking so, she was not sure she heard correctly. Then Miss Reamer took a snow-white cap from her desk and pinned it to Cherry's hair. She gave it an approving pat.

"Congratulations, Miss Ames," she said. "If you keep up the high standard you have set yourself, you should be one of our finest nurses. You are a credit to the school."

Cherry had to grip the edge of the desk, the shock of it all was so sudden. She hadn't failed! She was still in the school—and not merely that! She was now a full-fledged student nurse. Second highest in the class . . . a credit to the school . . . She was so happy that she felt as if she would burst. She groped for words.

"I— Thank you, Miss Reamer—I'm so glad, so——"

"Of course you are. And we are too."

"I love this hospital." Miss Reamer nodded. Cherry asked suddenly, "Did Dr. Wylie——?"

Miss Reamer's eyes twinkled. "Dr. Wylie does not report on probationers, but he happened to mention to me that you take criticism well. And Miss Craig sent in a very nice report, saying that you make a real effort to learn." Cherry listened almost unbelievingly and melted with gratitude. They were not ogres—they were only trying to teach and help her! There was no rancor, for the beloved hospital was bigger than any of them. The Superintendent of Nurses said in a softer voice, "Perhaps you did not know that Miss Craig trained at this very same hospital, when it was just one small building and when she was your age. And she had her troubles, too."

Cherry felt the tears dangerously near the brink now, so she gasped out, "Thank you!" and escaped. In the hall, she practically fell into Ann's and Gwen's waiting arms.

"Oh, Cherry, I knew you'd get it! I knew there must be a mistake!"

"But of course, you silly, of course you'd get it—congratulations—look at her in her cap!"

They hugged each other, and all of Cherry's misery fell away as if it had never happened. She had her cap! She reached up and gently touched it. Dr. Wylie had actually praised her! Miss Craig had approved her work!

And Jim Clayton, the darling, had personally gone to her rescue. He did care something about her. She remembered what he had said to her that awful afternoon.

"You'll make a nurse, Cherry—a good nurse."

He was right. She had won her cap and she would win through till she had the graduate's broad black velvet ribbon on that cap. This was only the happy beginning. Cherry knew it now.

~~~~~~

CHAPTER VIII

Emergency!

MAYBE THE NEW CAP HAD SOMETHING TO DO WITH IT.
That proud new cap, perched on Cherry's black curls,
with her red cheeks and black-diamond eyes ablaze under it. Maybe it was because Vivian Warren had stood
ill-at-ease at Cherry's door one evening and said, "I
want to congratulate you—and to thank you." Or maybe
it was being measured for bibs and students' striped
blue and white dresses, and—glory of glories—those
dashing capes!

At any rate, the next month, December, was one of
the happiest Cherry had ever galloped through. Outside,
the world froze into a fairyland of ice and traceries in
the glistening snow. Inside, the great hospital was
busier and gayer and dearer than ever.

"Where're you going?" Gwen cried, tumbling into
Cherry's room the evening the class had received its

new assignments. Everyone was too excited to study much tonight. Gwen waved a slip of paper. "I've drawn Skin—golly, all those smelly ointments!"

"The sniffy Miss Jones," Ann teased, coming in behind her. She settled herself in the rocker, remarking, "I might as well sit down while I can. Think of me when you're snug in your beds. I've got night duty." Ann groaned, but her dark blue eyes shone with satisfaction.

Cherry passed the box of fudge Midge had made and sent her. When the girls had their mouths full, she broke her own news as nonchalantly as possible. "I'm off to Emergency Ward."

They sputtered. "You lucky thing!" Ann cried. "Honestly, did you ever hear of anyone so lucky! The most exciting place in the hospital!"

And Gwen said rapturously, "Life at first hand! Bus! And all those handsome internes!" She pretended to swoon but not before she had popped another piece of fudge into her mouth. "Life and ambulance bus!"

Cherry tried to look modest. "Well, life, as you put it, Miss Jones, may turn out to be nothing more exciting than sprained thumbs, but I sort of expect that——"

Just then there came a warning pounding from the floor. Cherry hastily opened a notebook. Gwen grabbed a physiology book, while Ann strewed papers and pencils around the room. When the house mother opened the door a minute later, she saw three student nurses deeply engrossed in study. Gwen squirmed a little, for she had sat down on the box of fudge.

The minute the house mother had gone, Cherry stamped on the floor, explaining, "That's to say thanks to Mai Lee." Then she climbed up on a chair and hammered on the ceiling. "Marie Swift's over me." The girls brought out the fudge, plus a fashion magazine, and—just this one night—ignored such things as physiology in favor of Cherry's marvelous luck.

Emergency Ward was undeniably exciting. Even the appearance of the place was exciting. Situated on the street level of the hospital, it ran the whole length of one wing, and faced a large courtyard where ambulances came screeching up night and day. There were two big wards, Men's and Women's, and all around them, a maze of small operating rooms, recovery rooms, and examination rooms. The newest equipment in the hospital was here, including the fabulous Iron Lung. Outside the wards, there were waiting and interviewing rooms, and an emergency clinic. Telephone operators, policemen, ambulance drivers, maids with steam wagons of food, nurses, doctors, patients—people streamed in and out all the time.

And what people! All ages, sizes, shapes, nationalities, and conditions, some shrieking over a scratch, some carried in broken and bloody from an automobile accident and some telling Cherry their life stories as she struggled to take only their medical histories. It seemed as if the whole teeming life of the city spilled over into the Emergency Ward.

Cherry remarked on it, during her first few startling days there, to Ruth Schwartz, the E.W. head nurse. Miss Schwartz was young but she had the calm, responsible, unshakeable poise of a matriarch. Her solemn face and brooding eyes, Cherry soon learned, were a "dead pan" for an hilarious sense of humor.

"If you think this is the best show E.W. can put on," Miss Schwartz assured Cherry, "wait until the streets freeze over. This ward, you know, has twenty-nine beds. Last winter we squeezed in *sixty*-nine beds. One side of the room was Medical, the other side Surgical, as usual. It was a regular circus in here. Some of us worked two days and two nights without rest," she said, with no more ado than if she had said she had coffee for breakfast that morning. She predicted, "Just wait till the streets freeze over!"

The reception room nurse came hurrying in. "Miss Schwartz! A man out here—probably brain concussion. Hurry!"

As she calmly sped after the nurse, Miss Schwartz looked back at Cherry with a wry combination of a sigh and a twinkle. "They've frozen over!"

A minute later two orderlies brought in a man moaning on a stretcher. Occasionally he cried out pitifully. Miss Schwartz did not show a flicker of pity or concern.

"This bed, more blankets," she ordered. "Miss Post, will you call Dr. Jackson immediately? Oxygen tank, Miss Ames, please roll it over. Heating pads. Quick now, lift him. Good work, Miss Ames."

Almost indifferent, she seemed. But, lifting, Cherry found that the head nurse's hands had gone ice-cold and her eyes were tense with worry.

"She looks and acts so hard-boiled," Cherry thought, as she worked with her, "but I'll bet she's one of the kindest people here."

By the time Dr. "Ding" Jackson arrived, Miss Schwartz, with Cherry's help, had made the patient comfortable, arranged serums and oxygen should the doctor want them quickly, got a report from the ambulance interne, and prepared a chart.

Dr. "Ding" was a sandy-haired, lanky young man with a New England drawl. He frowned as he examined the suffering man. "Looks like he's on a one-way street, and going in the wrong direction."

"We'll just take his foot out of those clouds," Miss Schwartz said sternly. Cherry thought she looked angry enough to speak to St. Peter personally about saving this patient.

But after Dr. Jackson and two orderlies had wheeled the man to a private room, Cherry had a shock. Miss Schwartz came sauntering back wearing a fresh apron. She patted the pert bow into place, humming.

"Does it look all right from in back?" she said to Cherry. "I do like a crisp clean apron, and a big bow."

Cherry looked from the bow to Miss Schwartz's casual face and gasped out, "But that poor man—he's in a bad way! A bow!" Then she caught herself, "I beg your pardon."

Miss Schwartz's alert eyes softened. "Don't you think I'm praying for him as hard and fast as I can? But a nurse must translate her pity into action. And we have to keep calm and cheerful for the other patients." She smiled as if she were a thousand years old. "Working on Emergency Ward makes you a realist."

"Makes you tough?" Cherry asked hesitantly.

"Goodness, no." Miss Schwartz shook her head emphatically. "A tough nurse is a bad nurse. I mean—let's see——"

But at that moment the reception room nurse popped in again. "Women's side. Looks like a heart attack. May be a suicide attempt."

Cherry felt a cold sensation in the pit of her stomach. She followed Miss Schwartz into the Women's Ward. Sweat broke out on her upper lip. The unshakeable head nurse had not turned a hair.

On the bed lay a beautiful blonde young woman, wrapped in a luxurious fur coat. She was still and white and cold. Her hat had fallen off, and her hair fell across her lovely face.

"Oh, the poor thing," Cherry whispered, brushing the soft fair hair off the pale cheeks. "The poor little thing."

"Save your pity," Miss Schwartz snapped. "Please phone the Intake desk and ask them to send us this patient's purse."

Cherry went to the ward phone, thinking, "She is hard-boiled at that." When she returned, the young woman's large eyes had fluttered open and she struggled to speak. Cherry could not quite make it out. "He doesn't— No, no——"

They worked together for several minutes over the young woman. A maid brought in the patient's purse. Miss Schwartz examined its contents and handed Cherry a tube of nitroglycerin pills from the woman's handbag.

"Do you know what these mean?"

Cherry's eyes widened. Nitroglycerin—she could hear the instructor's voice and see the textbook page as memory flashed into place. "Disrupts heart action! Oh! Miss Schwartz! That means she tried to kill herself!" She looked down at the struggling woman.

"Does it?" Miss Schwartz said indifferently and began to administer a counter-serum. "Miss Ames, I am leaving the patient in your care." She gave a few instructions, turned on her heel, and strolled away.

"She's as hard as nails," Cherry changed her mind angrily, looking after her.

A little color slowly drained back into the patient's

delicate face. Cherry was chafing her cold hands when three men appeared at the door of the ward. Cherry rose to bar their way, but Miss Schwartz miraculously turned up.

"No reporters," the head nurse said firmly. "Sorry. Really we can't——"

Cherry turned back to her patient and found the young woman sitting bolt upright on the bed. Her violet eyes were no longer fluttering, but blazing. "And why can't I see reporters?" she demanded. "When Linda Royce tries to commit suicide, her fans call that news!" She was still a little giddy from the nitroglycerin, but she declared loudly, "Nurse! You can't cheat me out of my publicity!"

Miss Schwartz got the whole troupe out quickly and with deft tact. Cherry just stood there and blinked.

Miss Schwartz came over to her, as cool as ever. "You forgot one little word," she said, her eyes dancing. "Nitroglycerin disrupts heart action *temporarily*. That tells you at once the patient is trying to get sympathy or publicity or avoid some responsibility or make somebody sorry by putting on an alarming act. It never works, either." Cherry looked at Ruth Schwartz with mute apology in her eyes. The young head nurse grinned back at her. "Now you'd better have a glass of milk, Miss Ames. You're looking a little pale."

Cherry sat down alone in a deserted examination room and drank her milk thoughtfully. Miss Schwartz was a revelation. Cherry recalled now that she and Miss Mac were close friends. That was not surprising. The two nurses were much different on the surface—the one solemn, the other gay, and they were of different nationalities—still, both young women had the same devotion to nursing, the same zest for people, the same open-eyed sense of humor.

"Ruth Schwartz says her poise is just an Emergency Ward product," Cherry chuckled to Ann and Gwen, telling them about the Linda Royce episode later.

The trio was in Ann's room, really studying this snowy late afternoon. Besides some of the old studies, they now had classes in ethics, psychology, and pharmacology.

"Wonder whether we'll ever be as good nurses as that," Ann said as she labored over a chemical formula.

"Well, I know one thing," Gwen declared. "Getting out of the probie stage and getting into blue and white *and* a cap has done my self-confidence an awful lot of good." She put down her book and ran her fingers through her red hair. "And I know something else, in case anyone wants to hear it."

"Speak up," Cherry encouraged, "you know we love you."

"We hang on your every word," Ann assured her.

Gwen made a face at them, then continued seriously, "Now that we have our caps, haven't you noticed something different about the doctors and the older nurses?

They trust us! We're no longer nitwits to them. Which reminds me, Cherry, how's your Dr. Jim Clayton?"

Cherry stuttered and felt her face turn pink under their teasing eyes. "*My* Dr. Clayton? He's not mine— Of course I like him but it's nothing—" She had not dreamed that Gwen and Ann might guess how much she liked that young man. "Why, I don't know what you mean!" she added unconvincingly.

"Uh huh," Ann said sympathetically. "I don't suppose you'd be interested to know that he's going down to Emergency Ward to take care of a tuberculosis case."

The tuberculosis case arrived before Dr. Clayton did. A dirty, cross, skinny old lady who refused to let Cherry get her into a nightgown for X-ray. Her clothes were ragged and filthy, faded past recognition, sagging in a witch's folds. She stood arguing with Cherry in one of the dressing rooms.

"These clothes are mine, the only clothes I got in the world, and I ain't letting anyone steal them!" she told Cherry accusingly.

"But it's for X-ray—you know, inside information," Cherry coaxed.

"I don't trust these here hospitals!" the old lady scolded. "Why, I know somebody once who died in a hospital! That proves hospitals are no good, don't it?"

Cherry sighed. She was acquainted by now with this ignorant attitude. She knew, too, that only as far back as the 1860's hospitals really had been terrible places, where patients were lucky to come out alive, and resorted to only by the helpless poor. But that was before antiseptics and sterilization had been discovered, and before Florence Nightingale had founded the first training school for nurses. Perhaps it was this outworn reputation that stuck in the back of this old woman's mind. Whatever it was, Cherry and even Miss Schwartz argued in vain.

"All right," the head nurse told her in despair. "You can be X-rayed with all your clothes on. Gloves and overshoes, too, if you like."

"Watch her," Miss Schwartz warned Cherry under her breath. "Patients sometimes try to run away." But the trip to X-ray went off safely.

When Cherry showed Dr. Jim Clayton the X-ray plates later, he burst out laughing.

"What's funny about tuberculosis?" Cherry chided him. "I thought the poor woman hadn't a chance."

Dr. Clayton looked down at her, his warm brown eyes still full of laughter. "Don't believe in bogies, Cherry. Tuberculosis *is* curable, if you catch it early enough, and this old lady has come in in time. She came in to have an infected finger treated and fortunately we heard that cough. We can save her years of suffering and give her a peaceful old age. But—but—" He burst out laughing again.

"X-ray insisted she take off those filthy clothes. The nurse peeled off layer after layer, like an onion. And do you know what? In the hems and seams of that old woman's clothes, even in her stocking tops, she had sewn rolls of bills! A walking bank!" Dr. Clayton chuckled. "A miser, I guess. We get one every so often. Well, Social Service will send her upstairs to Dr. Wylie and charge her whatever she can afford."

Cherry's mouth and eyes opened at the same time. Dr. Clayton gently yanked one black curl. "You're learning, aren't you, youngster?"

Cherry smiled and felt better.

One rushed morning, when all the beds were full and the whole E.W. staff were working like demons and Cherry was wishing she were triplets, Dr. "Ding" Jackson strode in and said, "Urgent. Come on." Cherry was in the midst of giving the patients their morning care, but she turned over the task to the other student nurse immediately.

"A third-degree burn," he explained briefly as Cherry hurried to keep up with his long, lanky strides. "One of those home accidents. A hot water boiler exploded in his face. He won't have any face for the rest of his life, unless we act fast. We'll clean it up now and pray that Dr. Sutton can do a series of plastic surgeries later. May have to come back to the hospital at intervals for two or three years."

Cherry steeled herself to look upon not a face but a painful red pulp. "How old is he?" Cherry asked as they wheeled around a corner, just missing a stretcher.

No face for the rest of his life, "Ding" had said. "He's seven years old."

Cherry gasped. "His—his eyes?" she whispered.

"No, he won't be blind. But we mustn't let Winky grow up disfigured. It would warp his soul as well as his body." Dr. "Ding" brushed back his sandy forelock unhappily. "He's horribly frightened, Miss Ames. And —he has no mother."

Cherry was glad then that she was a nurse. Even a student nurse. Glad to the very bottom of her heart.

At the door, she faced Dr. Jackson. "Let me go in alone." He nodded.

The boy's figure looked very small in the high hospital bed. His face was swathed in medicated gauze. Only two round, bright blue eyes flickered, birdlike, in what once must have been a lively little face. Cherry suddenly remembered her own brother, when Charlie was just as young, and how he always pretended bluffly to be afraid of nothing.

Cherry went over to the side of the bed. "Hello, Winky," she said softly. "So you've come to pay us a visit here at the hospital. I'll bet your teacher is surprised you aren't in school this morning."

The childish eyes looked up at her forlornly, waiting for her to say more. Winky could not talk.

Cherry swallowed hard and laid her hand lightly on his shoulder. "We're your friends here and we're going to take good care of you, Winky. You're going to get well. You know that, don't you? And you'll have loads of fun here. I'll play games with you and you shall have your own private radio and——"

She stopped, halted by the expression in the little boy's eyes. He looked up at her trustingly enough, but he was pleading with her, anxiously asking her something. Suddenly she understood. The child realized his face was burned away.

"And you are going to be just as nice-looking as ever. You won't look a bit different, you'll be the same old Winky, just like you always were. Honestly."

Such a look of relief came into his eyes! And then they relaxed and closed for a moment. Cherry felt something plucking at her hand. Winky's grimy small hand had found hers and curled tightly around her cool fingers.

The door flew open and a heavy-set man, apparently Winky's father, burst in past the doctor and the head nurse. He was hatless, his hair was flying, and he was weeping. "He'll be a freak—no one will want to look at him—" he sobbed. "He's better off dead——!"

So that was where Winky had got his fear! Cherry whirled the man around, and Miss Schwartz and Dr. Jackson seized him and pulled him out into the hall.

"Never offer a patient worry or pity or even too much sympathy," Miss Schwartz's voice echoed faintly in Cherry's memory. But all Winky's hope had died again. Cherry went back to the bed and stubbornly, patiently, fought with the child's fear. She explained very simply, and entirely honestly, how the wonderful surgeon would heal his face. She told him of other people who were severely burned and who got well because they were brave and cooperated with the doctor. With both his stubby hands tight in hers, Cherry promised him that he too would recover. Winky was finally satisfied enough to close his eyes and at last he went off into an uneasy sleep. Cherry knew he believed in her, and through her, in himself. She gently withdrew her hand from his uncurling fist and tiptoed away from the bed.

She had barely stepped into the glistening corridor when Dr. Jim Clayton hailed her. "Please send up the tuberculosis patient's Intake report to Dr. Wylie at once."

"Miss Ames! Miss Ames!" the head nurse called. "Your fracture patient is asking for you. Don't forget to look at Mrs. Knox's dressing, too."

"How's Winky?" Dr. Jackson asked, coming up. "I'll want you to be on hand when we feed him by intravenous infusion."

"Miss Ames! Miss Ames! Telephone. Take it on the south ward!"

"Yes!" said Cherry. "Yes! Yes! Yes!" Laughing a little in her bewilderment, she broke into a run. Never before had she felt so thoroughly alive! "What a day!" she thought in exhilaration. She grabbed the receiver and said crisply into the phone, "Emergency Ward, Miss Ames speaking."

"Why, Cherry! You don't have to speak that way to me!" said a woman's voice. The voice sounded far away and poignantly familiar. Cherry was startled and puzzled. One of her former patients? A patient's relative? Who else could be phoning her? And then——

"Oh, darling, it's *you!*" Cherry shouted into the phone. "Mother!"

They laughed together over the miles.

"I was worried, Cherry," her mother said. "Your letters have been so brief recently. Are you unhappy there? Or not feeling well? Is it too much for you?"

Cherry simply roared. "Oh, no, just the opposite! Mother, it's wonderful—marvelous—" Winky, winning her cap, and chumming with Ann and Gwen, and the excitement of Emergency Ward, and Christmas "Candle Walk" coming— Cherry wanted to pour out all this to her mother.

"I'll write you all about it soon!" she cried into the phone. "And I just want to tell you this—I've never been happier in my whole life!"

CHAPTER IX

Candle Walk

CHERRY TURNED OVER IN BED AND LUXURIOUSLY snuggled into the pillows. She was busy thinking. It was still dark outside her window, quiet in the Nurses' Residence—too early to get up, thank goodness. This was the only chance she had to think over all that had happened. She still felt out of breath from her three weeks on Emergency Ward. She had suddenly been transferred, ten days ahead of time, because Bone Deformities Ward lost a nurse and needed someone in a hurry. T.S.O. considered Cherry good enough to meet this emergency. So here she was already on the new ward—Bone Deformities. High time she took a few minutes to catch up with herself!

There was Winky, for one thing. Cherry was still a little stunned. Winky was better now, much better, eating and talking. She had popped into his room every day, sometimes only for a minute, but she had come faithfully. The round, bright blue eyes smiled gaily at her now, for she and Winky were fast friends. When she came in to tell him she was unexpectedly being transferred upstairs, the little boy looked woebegone. Then he set up an awful howl.

"If you go, I'm going too!" he insisted.

His R.N. came running in to see what the awful noise was about. "But, Winky dear," the registered nurse explained, "Miss Ames is going to a part of the hospital where they don't fix faces."

"Why can't they fix my face just as good in one room as in another?" Winky demanded.

Cherry interposed tactfully and hastily, "Your own nurse will take very, very good care of you, right here in your own room."

"I don't want anybody to take care of me but Miss Cherry!" Winky wailed. "I'm going with Miss Cherry!"

And he wore himself out insisting and fretting until Dr. Sutton had to be summoned. The surgeon, when he learned that Cherry was going to Orthopedic, was doubtful about sending a plastic surgery case to a completely unrelated ward. But the little boy pleaded so earnestly and so long that finally Dr. Sutton said:

"We-ell, it's all wrong, but I guess we'll have to put Winky in a private room just off the Orthopedic Ward."

So Winky was carried up to Bone Deformities, of all places, making it inconceivably inconvenient for the plastic surgeon, the assisting doctor, his own R.N., and balling up all the hospital records and procedures, but close to his beloved Cherry.

Cherry wiggled her toes reflectively. Her feet still ached a little. They ached not from working, but from dancing half the night at the Fall Term dance. It seemed funny to go to a party, not in her prettiest dress, but in a fresh uniform, and Cherry had worried about not looking glamorous enough to attract many partners. Apparently Dr. Jim Clayton liked the combination of blue and white with red cheeks and black hair. Though he danced with lovely Miss Baker until she had to leave, after that he danced almost exclusively with Cherry. Dr. "Ding" Jackson paid her a lot of attention, too, and a whole swarm of internes she knew only by sight until that night. There had been punch and sandwiches, and Gwen's red head bobbing merrily at the front of the conga line, and Ann talking earnestly in a corner to an unidentified young doctor. But most of all, there had been Jim Clayton.

Cherry was just beginning to think melting thoughts when the rising bell clanged like a dozen fire engines and practically hurled her back into Tuesday morning, six A.M., and plenty of work ahead.

"There's plenty to do on Orthopedic," Cherry thought as she came hurrying in smiling as warmly as she could at the helpless crippled patients. She pitied them. The women here lay rigid in their casts, broken-backed, or unable to stir their paralyzed bodies under the heated "domes" which arched across their beds. It was a brave ward, full of hope that with months or even years of treatment and courage they might some day walk. It was a ward that made Cherry thankful for her own sound legs and good straight back. The women called cheerful "Good mornings" to her, even though the December morning was gray and snowing.

Cherry took around breakfast trays to her own four patients, assisting Mary Miller who could not feed herself, and gave them morning care. Then she counted aloud while the two patients who could and must perform passive exercises lying prone in their beds, painfully but obediently flexed knees and fingers. After that, Cherry stole a minute to look in on Winky in his new room. He had had his breakfast and had dropped off to sleep again, his tousled bandaged head cocked on one shoulder.

In the hall someone hailed her. It was Bertha Larsen, her round face beaming. She came up and put her sturdy arm around Cherry in genuine affection. "You know what I heard?" she said in her sing-song voice. "You will be so glad!"

"What is it?" Cherry gave Bertha's plump white hand a squeeze.

"Such good news for you! Like a Christmas present! They say Dr. Wylie has been asked to go to the battle fronts and may leave here. Now, wouldn't that be nice?"

Cherry bit her crimson lip, trying not to laugh. "Oh, Bertha, you mustn't say such things—even if you feel that way. We both might be seriously misunderstood."

Bertha's honest face clouded. "But it's true, isn't it?"

"I'd be greatly relieved," Cherry admitted dryly, "if Dr. Wylie were to disappear out of my life."

"Dr. Wylie reminds me of a stubborn bad-tempered old cow we have back on our farm," Bertha remarked placidly. "I think I'll tell him so some time."

"You'd better not!"

Bertha folded her arms across her buxom figure. "A good scolding might do him good. It works fine with our cow."

They saw the supervisor coming and hastily parted. Cherry was still trying to sober her face when she reentered the ward. Perhaps Bertha was right at that. Perhaps Dr. Wylie might have more respect for her if she fought back. Unfortunately, in his dual role of senior surgeon and administrator, that stern gentleman had his sharp nose into every nook and cranny of the hospital. He had a case on Orthopedic now, too. He had not discovered Winky up here yet, for both Winky and Cherry had barely moved in, but when he did, Cherry fully expected trouble. However, thinking of Dr. Wylie as cousin to the Larsen's cow cheered her considerably.

Cherry hurried through her ward duties and her studies on Orthopedic with an eager sense of expecting something to happen. Something nice, from the happy way she felt. Maybe it was Christmas excitement in the air that made her tingle inside. Or perhaps it was her approaching birthday, which fell—most unfairly, Cherry always thought, from the angle of presents—the day before Christmas. This would be her first birthday and first Christmas away from home, and she felt a little forlorn about it. Well, this Christmas she would think about her patients, not about herself.

It was wonderful how Christmas brought them renewed interest and courage. Even Mary Miller was able, for the first time, to turn herself around in bed, so eager was she to watch when the nurses dragged a great fir tree into the ward. Cherry and the other girls set it up between the windows, amid much puffing and panting and laughter. The nurses brought out the decorations they had bought.

"The blue star has to go on top!" Mary cried from her bed.

"The tinsel's too high," another patient contributed. "And look, there's room there for another red doo-dad!"

They worked three afternoons on it until the tree shone in glory.

"Bells and e-stars and e-sugar canes!" marveled the twisted little Puerto Rican woman. *"Madre de Dios,* Mees Ames, ees the most beautiful tree never have I saw!"

The tree *was* beautiful. Winky must see it. Cherry ran in to his lonesome little room to get him. His eyes grew rounder and rounder as she told him of the wonderful tree and bundled him carefully into a wheel chair.

"I have a tree all my own," he said gamely as she tucked blankets about him. "See?" he pointed to a tiny tree on his bedside table. "You know who gave me that? My daddy. Maybe I won't have no more Christmases."

The little boy looked up at Cherry worriedly for reassurance.

She drew in her breath in sudden fury. They had explained and explained to Winky's father. Why did he have to keep acting as if he didn't expect Winky to get well? "That's not so, Winky. You're going to have so many Christmases you won't be able to count them all."

"You sure?"

"I'm so sure," Cherry bent over him, "that let's you and I make a date right now for next Christmas and the Christmas after that."

"Okay. You won't forget by next year and next next year, will you?"

"I could as soon forget you as my own people," Cherry thought fiercely. "And as for your hysterical father——"

Her thought was interrupted the moment she wheeled Winky into the ward. Winky was an extremely popular young man. The women halted their exclamations to listen to his rapturous sigh as he beheld the Christmas tree. He looked a long moment, his eyes shining, and then he said one breathless word: "Jiminy!"

Out of the happy hush came a cold voice.

"What is this case doing on Orthopedic?" demanded Dr. Wylie. He turned and stared at small Winky, then walked over to Cherry, his coat flapping like the harsh grating of his own voice. "Miss Ames! I've had enough trouble with you before! This child isn't a bone case, is he?"

"No, sir," Cherry whispered, "he's a plastic surgery case. I just brought him in to see the tree."

"There's a tree on Plastic Surgery. I presume you know that. Take him back where he belongs! Christmas is no excuse for disrupting hospital routine!"

"But he belongs here, sir."

Dr. Wylie's eyebrows went up and Cherry talked as fast as she could. There was a dense silence from the rest of the ward as Dr. Wylie absorbed this strange infraction of rules.

"So you're to blame," he snapped, his steely eyes boring into Cherry, "as usual. So it's your fault."

The hot blood rose to her cheeks. "Cow," she mumbled. "Cow!"

"What's that?" Dr. Wylie demanded sharply.

Cherry planted her feet firmly and dug her fists in her pockets. "I said yes! I'm to blame! It's my fault! If making a patient like you is a fault!" She was so angry she had no time to be afraid. "And if that's a fault, sir, I'm not at all sorry!"

Dr. Wylie drew up his stocky tense figure and his whole aquiline face seemed to throw off electric sparks. "That will do!" he roared at her. "Take this boy back to his room at once and don't let me hear any more of your impertinence!" He choked in inarticulate rage.

Cherry swung the wheel chair around, thinking furiously, "Of all the undeserved bawlings-out! He's down on me, that's all! He doesn't even try to understand! He's just got it in for me!"

Dr. Wylie could choke himself into a froth or he could go off to the battle fronts or he could turn into a cow. She refused to worry about the incident. Strangely enough, she felt relieved and confident, and calmly went about her business. The afternoon fell into its usual grooves. Cherry gave her patients dinner, said good night to Winky, and went on downstairs for her own dinner. That gay and tingling feeling had bubbled up again. After all, it was nearly Christmas and her birthday.

After dinner, Cherry's whole class retired, giggling, for the Candle Walk rehearsal. They locked themselves in the basement and mysteriously made as little noise as possible. The last few days before Christmas flew by and only those rehearsals in the shadowy basement, with the girls' white faces massed together like flowers, seemed real to Cherry.

Late one afternoon, just four days before Christmas, when Cherry was in her room making herself neat and fresh for dinner, one of the nurses from T.S.O. rapped at her door.

"Someone to see you, Miss Ames."

Cherry flew over to Spencer and into the lounge. She knew she had been waiting for something! There, sitting stiffly on the sofa, all dressed up in their best clothes, were Dr. Joe and Midge! Cherry fell into their arms and then stood back to have a good look at them. Dr. Joe looked as frail and absent-minded as ever, his thatch of gray hair falling in his eyes, and a little uncomfortable without his white laboratory coat.

"How is it going, Cherry?" He looked at her keenly. "I want to hear all the details."

"You shall, Dr. Joe! But look at Midge! She's grown!"

"Did you like my fudge? How's Charlie's watch? Can I meet Ann and Gwen? How many patients do you have? Are you in love yet?"

"Whoa!" Cherry laughed. "How long are you going to be in town?"

"Only this evening and tomorrow morning when I see the Administrative Board about my drug."

Cherry's face fell. She knew she could not get the morning off. She hurried to T.S.O. and secured permission to go out for dinner with her visitors.

It seemed strange to be dining out, in a real dress, at a downtown restaurant. But there was nothing strange about being once more with Dr. Joe and Midge. They had so much talking to catch up on—Cherry's hospital adventures, Dr. Joe's experiments, Midge's doings in and out of school, love and news of Cherry's family, Hilton's new clinic now being built, and the three kittens Tookie had produced. Then Dr. Joe told Cherry the reason for his visit.

"Not that seeing you isn't enough reason," he said, smiling his gentle smile. "But I have reached a point in my experiments with the new anaesthetic where I must have a chance to test it or—or—well, or I just can't go on. I've brought it with me and I'm hoping—" he nervously fingered his napkin, "that Spencer Hospital will test it. They would test it—if they do—in their laboratory first, of course. My own is small and limited, I cannot test it properly. Then, too, it should be tested on animals and I have no facilities for that. Then, finally, I hope very much the hospital will test it on volunteers and, if it is satisfactory, use it for patients. Cherry, I *know* this derivative compound can save lives! It will advance surgery, and prevent pain—if only——"

"—if only the hospital will believe in you and give you a hearing," Cherry finished. She looked at Dr. Joe thoughtfully. His years of lonely work, his willing poverty, his discouragement—of those, typically, he had not said a word. She asked hesitantly, "Have they given you any hint—do you think they'll accept your drug for experiment—or perhaps they haven't said . . ."

Dr. Joe shook his head. "They've said no. I'm here to try to get them to change their minds. But I'm not very hopeful."

"Oh." Cherry exchanged a worried glance with Midge.

"But I will do one thing!" Dr. Joe was speaking with unaccustomed fire. "I will insist on leaving a few grams of the anaesthetic in the laboratory here! Then, in case they change their minds, or in case there is an emergency, the drug will be in the hospital."

His words struck Cherry hard. She would remember that Dr. Joe's precious new drug was in the laboratory.

"Well, I'm going to be cheerful this evening anyhow!" Midge said stoutly. "Dad has to meet an old doctor friend this evening, so can I come back to the hospital with you, Cherry, and meet Ann and Gwen?"

"Of course," Cherry said.

In Cherry's room that evening, Midge not only met Ann and Gwen, but Bertha and Mai Lee and Josie and Vivian and Marie Swift as well. Cherry squeezed nine girls in her tiny room and made a party of it, with ice cream and cookies she had bought on the way home, and Midge as guest of honor. Midge was so impressed by the uniforms and the girls' nonchalant professional chatter that she sat shy and silent. "You're only about four or five years older than I am but you seem so grown-up!" Cherry heard her confide to Ann.

"That's because our lives have a focus, instead of just

drifting," Ann explained. "Deciding on a career, and taking the first steps toward it—well, that alone is enough to make you grown-up."

Midge knitted her brows. "Guess I'd better grow myself up then." As usual, she jumped grasshopper-fashion to another subject. "It's too bad about Cherry." Cherry, overhearing, held her breath.

"What's all this?" Gwen interrupted. "Has Cherry a secret sorrow?"

"Oh, yes." Midge nodded knowingly. Heaven alone knew what Midge was capable of saying. All the girls were listening now. "It's that trouble about her birthday, you know," she said regretfully. And she went on to explain that Cherry never got *both* Christmas and birthday presents "like normal people." The girls laughed, but they sympathized too.

Cherry was embarrassed. She would have scolded Midge, except that she was so glad to see her friend, and so sorry, later, to have to put her on the downtown bus and say good-by.

"Call me up tomorrow and let me know what the hospital says about the drug," Cherry told her anxiously.

"I will," Midge promised. "Good night!"

When the phone rang around noon on the ward, Cherry knew it was Dr. Joe.

"They said no, Cherry." His voice sounded old and terribly discouraged

Cherry said what she could to console and hearten him. But Dr. Joe was in no mood to talk. He told her he had left the drug in the hospital, anyway, and then said good-by.

Even this, however, could not dampen Cherry's spirits for long. The hospital sparkled with holiday gaiety, and the first-year students rehearsed frantically. Two days before Christmas, Cherry managed to get out long enough to buy Winky a water color set and a picture book to go with it. He was going home soon now and could take it with him. Later that afternoon, Cherry received presents from home. She knew she should not open them until the next day, but who could possibly wait?

When she woke up on the morning of her birthday, there they were where she had spread them all out over the furniture: a fluffy white nurse's sweater and a lacy slip from her mother, a fountain pen with her name on it from Dad, Charlie's imaginative gift of white handkerchiefs appliquéd with gay red cherries in the corner, and a huge box of candy from them all, and a book from Dr. Joe and a pincushion in the shape of a calico heart from Midge. Cherry blinked at her combination birthday-and-Christmas gifts sleepily and happily. The sun was shining too. "Extra-special bright for my birthday," Cherry said aloud. It looked as if it was going to be a good birthday, even though she was away from home.

There was a knock on her door. Cherry was surprised, for the rising bell had not yet rung. "It's only I," came Gwen's muffled voice and the door opened a crack.

Cherry sat up in bed, alarmed. "If you're up this early, you sleepy-top, something must be wrong!" She stared as Gwen staggered in in her bathrobe, sleepily hugging a big box.

"Happy Birthday, Merry Christmas," Gwen yawned. She smiled. "Here. I got you *two* presents. Midge broke my heart the other night."

"You didn't! Why, Gwen Jones! *Two!*" Cherry scrambled for the box while Gwen curled up on the foot of her bed and closed one eye. She pulled the lid off and there lay two rubbers.

"One for the right foot, other for—" Gwen yawned hugely "—left foot. Two. See?"

Cherry said doubtfully, "Well, I do need rubbers but——."

Gwen vaguely waved her aside and gave a low whistle. Cherry's room suddenly filled with sleepy girls in assorted pajamas, nightgowns, and robes, their hair tousled and faces flushed.

Ann babbled vaguely, "Two presents, we all want you to be normal—" and she dropped a small package on Cherry's stomach. Cherry found in it the prettiest pair of gloves she had ever seen. She put them on, sitting cross-legged in bed, and sat with her chin on one gloved hand, staring incredulously at her staggering sleep-drunk visitors.

"Two legs, two garters," Josie explained nervously. "Happy whatever-it-is." A shout of delight went up when Cherry, getting excited now, held up Josie's white satin garters.

"Got to close the door," Gwen moaned and got up. "Want to wake up the whole place?" She weaved to the door and collapsed happily again on the bed.

"*Two,* you see it, two!" Bertha was explaining earnestly to Cherry. "I baked it myself. In our little dinky kitchen at the end of the hall."

"Mm, luscious!" Cherry cried, holding up the two-layer cake for them all to admire. She lay back weakly. "How come you're all so good to me? I'm—what's that word?—I'm overwhelmed!"

Mai Lee's little ivory face was demure with mischief as she handed Cherry twin swans-down powder puffs. Marie Swift had brought two red velvet bows for Cherry's hair. When, last of all, Vivian stepped up to the bed, Cherry felt a real thrill. Vivian—giving for perhaps the first time in her life! Her face had lost its hardness, and pride showed there instead, as she pressed two gay, inexpensive, colored glass roosters into Cherry's hand. "They're fighting cocks," Vivian tried to joke. "You and I, I guess."

"I guess *not!*" Cherry said warmly and hugged her.

"I nearly forgot," Ann said. "This is from Winky."
It was a wobbly but unmistakable water color picture of
a black-haired, red-cheeked girl in a blue and white
striped dress.

"What a birthday!" Cherry said over and over. And
they all sat down on the floor and ate cake before breakfast.

That evening, Christmas Eve, their class assembled
in the basement. It was pitch black down there, and the
voices of older nurses and internes floated down to them
teasingly. Upstairs the patients waited expectantly for
the traditional Candle Walk. In the dark they groped
their way into one long single file. Each girl was dressed
in her freshest uniform and apron, and each girl carried
in her hand a single tall white candle. Then the Superintendent of Nurses, a lighted taper in her hand, came
down the stairs. Slowly, smiling, she went down the
long row of young women, lighting each candle, and
faces sprang into view.

Upstairs in the darkened hospital, the procession
wove its way, singing. The gleaming candles, the fresh
young faces in the long lighted line, the clear sweet
voices, went from ward to ward. They sang old Christmas songs, a hymn or two, and all the ringing carols.
Cherry sang with the rest, looking into the flame of her
candle as if it were the very heart of Christmas. The
ceremony was like a dedication, Cherry thought, in
which that long line of her classmates, ahead and be-

hind her, brought light into the dark where the sick and suffering lay. The patients' worn faces smiled back at them out of the flickering shadows.

When the last ward had been visited, when the last carol had been sung, one by one the candles were snuffed out. The girls found their way home arm-in-arm through the cold starry night. Cherry looked at the great white hospital under the stars of this holy night and thought:

"Now I really know the hospital spirit! Why it's the same thing as Christmas—Christmas all year round!"

CHAPTER X

Four A.M. Mystery

WHERE THE TIME WENT, CHERRY NEVER COULD FIGURE out. The world outside froze blankly white and stayed that way. Cherry stayed on Women's Orthopedic during January, where day melted into busy day, and squeezed in jaunts to town with Ann and Gwen between studying. Classes had stepped up—there were lectures and visits to the wards in medical and surgical clinics and the hilarious bandage class, where the girls took turns winding each other in yards and yards of gauze. Cherry earned her bandage scissors, and admired them hanging so professionally at her belt. Cherry felt much surer of herself now and had a good firm grip on her work. When she moved from Bone Deformities to Women's Surgical at the beginning of February, she went onto the new ward without a tremor. And she did very good work there.

Milestones stood out here and there in that whizzing stream of days. There was the dance the internes gave for the nurses on Washington's Birthday. Jim Clayton pointed to the decorations, and said, "Looks like it's your personal party, Cherry." And Cherry, clutching a papier-mâché axe, said, "I cannot tell a lie. It isn't." But it was a very good party—mostly, Cherry thought, because she danced so many dances with Jim Clayton.

Then there was Charlie's letter. Cherry had a shock as she read it late one night as she soaked herself luxuriously in a hot tub. Charlie wrote he was leaving the university to study flying. He hoped, eventually, to join the Army Air Force. Women too, he wrote, could join the Army Air Force. His letter was full of strange words like "ferrying" and "bomber command" and "B–17's" and "P–38's" and "logistics." Those words made Charlie seem very grown-up, rather far away, in a strange new world of his own choosing. "Well," Cherry thought, "I'm following my dream and now he's going to follow his. It would be funny if some day the Ames twins were to bump into each other professionally as nurse and flier." But her own work kept her so busy she had no time to wonder. Before she knew it, it was March and she had slid smoothly out of Women's Surgical and into Out-Patient.

Out-Patient was fun. This was the free clinic where hordes of people streamed in daily for care "on the spot." It made Cherry think of her lively days on Emergency Ward. She was learning about medicine, but she was also learning about people. Cherry picked up enough pidgin Italian to soothe a worried little dark-eyed mother, she persuaded a crotchety old man to walk without his habitual crutch, she calmed a terrified Jewish woman who was sure she was dying because the doctor had prescribed a dreaded medicine called castor oil. And still they came, more and more faces, till she came to know Mr. O'Sullivan, who came back to the clinic because he liked the friendly nurses, not because he had anything wrong with him. And the strange, lonely woman, who, they later discovered, tore off her fresh bandages at home so that her hand would not heal and she would be entitled to more attention. And the babies who sprouted like beans from week to week.

"It's like a perpetual vaudeville show," Cherry told Ann and Gwen, "with an all-star cast!" They were in the pint-size laundry rinsing out their stockings.

Gwen nodded. "I'm getting a taste of it on Emergency Ward, and do I love it! The only thing is—how are they ever going to keep me down on a ward after I've seen The Big Show?"

Ann shook out her stockings in exasperation. "Everyone gets a ticket but me. I get the dullest assignments!" She was on Men's Surgical again, with the icy Miss Craig for head nurse. They had been short a nurse there.

"You've had night duty," Cherry reminded her. "My tongue's hanging out for that."

"Well, put your tongue right back in. The only exciting thing that happened to me on night duty was falling asleep and letting the six A.M. toast burn to a crisp. You could have smelled it way over here."

"Oh, we did," Gwen assured her. "But maybe Cherry will draw chills and thrills when she gets night duty."

"It would be just her marvelous luck," Ann agreed.

Cherry bowed but she saw no night duty in sight. It came, however, not suddenly, but in easy tantalizing stages. The first mild day, when the calendar announced April, and they opened the doors of Out-Patient and a whiff of spring blew in, Cherry received her notice to move on to Men's Orthopedic.

Cherry had something new on Men's Orthopedic— relief duty for three evenings, while the rest of the week was devoted to regular day duty. Previously her eight-hour shift had been from seven A.M. to three P.M. Now she came on at three in the afternoon until eleven at night, then the night nurse took over. The night nurse remained, alone, until seven the following morning. Cherry would have night duty after a week or so of relief duty.

"It's supposed to prepare you for staying up all night, so they say," Cherry explained to Ann and Gwen, "but all it does to *me* is whet my appetite for dinner."

As relief duty nurse, she settled the patients for

sleep and stayed with them through the quiet evening, preparing the night order book or folding bandages, until the night nurse came in, full of authority and making Cherry a bit jealous. The night world of the hospital provoked Cherry's imagination—the patients asleep in the shadowy white beds and deep silence, the lone nurse moving with her flashlight like a sentinel, vague figures of house doctors and supervisors floating all the long night throughout the closely guarded hospital.

Something happened one evening that gave Cherry a turn and made her thoughtful. About ten o'clock, when the ward was sleeping peacefully, moans came from a far bed. Cherry located the man—he was an ether case.

"I'm in terrible pain!" he panted. "Please, nurse . . . help me! Give me something!" He lay rigid with agony.

Cherry looked down at the man's chart. The doctor had ordered morphine if needed. But he had had his quotient that afternoon. Cherry called the supervisor, who in turn called the interne. It was young Dr. Freeman, a quiet, steady, plain-faced man.

"We need something else," Dr. Freeman said. "I don't want to give him another shot of this. Wish there were something else I could give him. But what?"

He and Cherry stood looking down at the sweating man, unable to help him. That hurt Cherry down to the core. What else was there? And then Cherry happened to think of Dr. Joe's new drug, stored away in the laboratory downstairs. She told Dr. Freeman about it.

"But we can't use it, it hasn't been approved yet. More morphine won't do this man any good." The patient moaned dully. Dr. Freeman took a deep breath. "All right, Miss Ames, give him another sixth of morphine," he said reluctantly.

Cherry administered it. But before she went off duty, she had to report to Dr. Freeman that it had not helped much or for very long. Something else was needed. "Why don't they make up their minds on Dr. Joe's drug?" she thought angrily as she ran through the cold, early spring rain to the Nurses' Residence.

That, and the fact that tonight was her first night duty, troubled her so much the next afternoon that she sought out Dr. Jim Clayton. Actually, Cherry was proud to be entrusted with night duty so early in her training. She found him in the library, and they went out to the deserted reception room and sat down in the window seat to talk. A little timid sunshine deepened the rose of Cherry's cheeks and picked out laughing golden lights in Jim Clayton's brown eyes.

"I don't know why I always come running to you with my troubles," she confessed, "but——"

"Maybe it's because you like me." He looked at her

intently. "I hope so." Cherry was flustered for a moment because her heart beat so hard. "Well, go ahead, shoot. What's on the Ames mind today?"

Cherry told him what had happened the previous night. Jim Clayton nodded. Then she went on to tell him about Dr. Joe's discovery, how it could be used as a local anaesthetic to take the place of a drug. "Think what it would mean for soldiers!" Cherry said. "In a way, Dr. Joe discovered it because of the war." She explained that when the quinine supply was cut off, because the areas where quinine is grown had fallen into enemy hands, many researchers had set about looking for a quinine substitute—Dr. Joe among them. Like some others, he had found one, but more important, his substitute had a by-product. And it was in this by-product that he had stumbled across a revolutionary drug. "It's so new it hasn't even a name yet," Cherry said, "except for a long-drawn-out formula." She wrinkled her nose trying to recite it.

Dr. Jim Clayton whistled. "Pretty learned, you are. But no joking, it's wonderful. You look like a pretty girl and you talk like a professor."

"Stop teasing! Be serious."

"I am serious. You are pretty, you know. Told Miss Baker so. Go ask her if I didn't."

"What's got into you today?" Cherry demanded, and her dark eyes opened wide and wondering.

"Dunno. Maybe I'm in love." He looked at her with

a face bubbling with laughter. "Miss Ames, do you think I'm in love?"

She was startled. This was more than she was prepared for. "I—I think I'll go ask Miss Baker if you are." She ran off breathless and dimpling.

When Cherry reached the door of Marjory Baker's ward, she stood for a moment in the doorway watching the young golden-haired head nurse, moving gracefully from bed to bed. "If I were a man," Cherry thought, "I'd be in love with her."

But she had her own romantic worries. She caught Miss Baker alone at her desk. They chatted a little of this and that, then Cherry skillfully steered the conversation to the subject of Jim Clayton. She asked, as offhand as possible:

"I wonder if he really likes me? He's so sweet to me, and bucks me up when I get discouraged—do you think he——"

"Of course he likes you," Miss Baker smiled back. "He wouldn't go to all that trouble if he didn't. By the way, I heard about Sally Chase."

"Oh!" But Miss Baker was laughing about Sally Chase and treating her as if she were a child. Cherry thought of Jim Clayton's intent eyes and dropped another hint. "He told me he's in love."

Miss Baker looked strange. Then she looked at Cherry understandingly and squeezed her hand. "I'm not surprised," she whispered.

Cherry ran out of the ward as if all the bells in the world were ringing just for her. She floated, not walked, down the corridor, quite unaware of where she was going, when a firm hand seized her wrist.

"You look as if you've just won the sweepstakes," laughed Miss McIntyre.

"I'm going on night duty tonight for the first time and that's nearly as exciting," Cherry replied. She noticed that Miss McIntyre looked quite excited herself.

"I've just seen something absolutely amazing."

Cherry kept pace with Miss Mac's free sportswoman's stride. She had a hard time paying attention to Miss Mac's conversation, with all those imaginary bells pealing, until one word. Then it dawned on her that Miss Mac was talking about Dr. Joe's drug, not about the new probies who had just arrived.

"—a staff demonstration just now," she was saying. "And it works! The chemical laboratory has tested it. They've tried it out on white rats, and it worked beautifully on three patients who volunteered."

"Then we can use it right away!" Cherry said eagerly.

"No, not until it has been accepted by the Medical Board. To use it before would be a breach of medical ethics. But it's a shame there's so much medical red tape," Miss McIntyre said forthrightly. "The Board doesn't meet again until July and this is only April. Seems too bad, doesn't it? But there it is."

Yes, there it was. Cherry might fret and other anaes-thetics be inferior but there lay Dr. Joe's drug unused.

Cherry thought about it, and about Dr. Jim, that first long night she was alone as night nurse, in sole responsibility for a heavy ward full of helpless people. The sweet cool April air filled the darkened ward, and the shadows lay thick and still, as Cherry made the rounds of beds. Only the glow of the lamp on the head nurse's desk—her desk for the night—and the stab of light from her flashlight, focused for a moment on a face, showed her a dim world asleep here. The super-visor looked in so seldom and the corridors beyond were so hushed that Cherry thought eerily, "It feels like being on another planet." But she was not frightened, and to her surprise, she had no struggle to keep awake. Cherry sat down at her desk and filled out the night report and then folded gauze sponges.

At midnight a relief nurse came in. She told Cherry she would be available to help out on any ward that might be very busy at night. Cherry felt reassured to know this nurse was near by. Cherry politely walked her to the door and chatted with her for a few minutes.

When Cherry turned back into the ward, the moon had tilted and spilled great splashes of blue-white light on the floor. Again she moved softly from bed to bed, sure-footed, deft-handed, a white guardian. The same man for whom Dr. Freeman had prescribed morphine could not sleep tonight. He was in pain, he murmured, and Cherry saw his dim, drawn face on the pillow. **Dr.** Freeman had forbidden any more morphine. There was nothing she could give him, and she thought angrily of Dr. Joe's unused drug.

"I'll get you a glass of milk," she said helplessly. She went out to the tiny kitchen, and found it strange in night magic. After the man had drunk the milk, Cherry softly talked to him, telling any stories that came into her head, until he fell asleep from sheer exhaustion. She stood over his bed, shaking her head and wondering why the Medical Board could not meet sooner.

The night wore on. Cherry thought of all the desperate things that were supposed to happen to a lone nurse on night duty—patients getting delirious or trying to escape, sudden heart attacks, hemorrhages. "Don't believe in bogies," Jim Clayton had said to her once. She smiled, almost seeing his face smiling down at her. Well, she very nearly wished something exciting would happen. The supervisor looked in. That was the only break in the routine for several hours. Cherry began to feel drowsy, so she walked around the ward to keep awake. At four the ward began to get chilly and Cherry slipped into her woolly white sweater. Outside on the black lawn, a bird called, then went back to sleep. "He saw his mistake, I guess," Cherry thought. Three more hours to go. Three more hours of sleeping silence. It was a long night.

Cherry was indulging herself in thoughts of **Jim**

Clayton when she heard the elevator—the self-service elevator, curiously—and muffled voices in the hall. Who could be there at this hour? If they were sending her an emergency case, why had not Emergency Ward phoned up to tell her to get a bed ready? She sprang up from her desk and hurried to the door. This was very strange.

Someone was being brought in on a stretcher. Alongside the two orderlies marched two men in business suits and, recognizable even in these dense shadows, Dr. Wylie! Perhaps they were going to the private pavilion, which was around the corner. No, they were coming here. No, they weren't either. Cherry was mystified to see the motley procession stop in the corridor and wait for somebody or something. The elevator came up again and a man in an unidentifiable uniform whispered to Dr. Wylie. She saw Dr. Wylie glance at her sharply. The men discussed something in low voices, looking at her.

Cherry could not understand what was going on. Perhaps they did not want her to see them and she started to move away discreetly. But Dr. Wylie called, "Nurse! Miss Ames, isn't it? Wait there."

The next thing that happened puzzled her even more. Dr. Wylie went to the door marked "Broom Closet," took a key from his pocket and unlocked the door. Instead of the cleaning closet Cherry had always assumed was there, the door swung open to reveal in the moonlight a fully equipped hospital room with a bed, and a bathroom beyond. She stood rooted to the spot in amazement.

"Miss Ames!" Dr. Wylie whispered. He beckoned her to come. As Cherry stepped out into the hall, the two men in business suits and the man in uniform withdrew deeper into the shadows, so that she could not see their faces. But she felt their eyes studying her. The patient's face was half-hidden with a towel. What —who—was this?

"Anyone on your ward awake?" Dr. Wylie demanded under his breath.

"I don't think so, sir."

"Good. Where's Miss Hall?"

"I don't know any Miss Hall, sir. I never heard of her."

"No, you wouldn't at that. Go in there and remake the bed and bring heated blankets. Where the devil can she be? And Miss Ames!"

"Yes, Dr. Wylie?"

She could hear his taut breathing in the dark. "Not a word of this to anyone. You understand? Now hurry as fast as you can."

"Yes, sir," Cherry faltered. She ran into the room and flung open the window. The air was dry and stale, the room had been closed for a long time. Beyond the bathroom, she found, was another room and two closed doors. She remade the bed quickly and dashed about

the room wiping up the worst of the dust, then flew
out to heat blankets.

As she came out the door, the men's voices suddenly
halted and they preserved silence until she had passed.
What was this, anyway? Something terribly important,
judging by their secrecy. Cherry thought of gangsters
and heads of governments in a wild whirl as she hastily
prepared blankets. The two men in business suits did
not look like ordinary men, she thought, as she sped
back. They had a professional air—no, not exactly—
a commanding air.

The hall was empty now. She rapped softly on the
door. It opened a crack. Dr. Wylie looked through,
and beyond him Cherry saw a pile of airplane luggage.
She handed in the blankets.

"Will you want anything else, sir?" she whispered.

"No, thanks," he said gruffly. "Just one or two things.
If the number three rings on the call board, ignore it.
I'll have it disconnected. Don't let anyone in here. I'll
stay with the patient myself. If Miss Hall comes, tell
her to wait in my office, and let me know. She probably
won't come now before you go off duty, so don't worry
about that." He paused, thinking and frowning. Cherry
waited. She heard someone calling in the ward, but
still Dr. Wylie kept her.

"Is that all, sir?" she asked finally.

He looked at her and seemed to return from a long
way off. "Ames. Nurse. Oh, yes. Now see here, Miss

Ames. I cannot impress this on you too strongly." His face was very serious. "You are not to tell anyone— *anyone*—of what you have seen tonight, on pain of expulsion. And you are never to go into that room again."

He closed the door and the lock clicked. Cherry had just turned away, when the door opened again and Dr. Wylie's hawk face darted out at her.

"And, Miss Ames!"

"Yes, sir," Cherry quavered, wondering how much more her shaking knees could survive.

"Wipe that rouge off your face!"

Cherry did not know whether to laugh or cry.

~~~~~~

CHAPTER XI

The Forbidden Room

"THE POOR SUFFERING LITTLE THINGS," ANN GASPED. "Oh, what agony those babies are in!"

"Don't tell me *we* looked as forlorn and scared and helpless as that only a few months ago!" Gwen said.

Cherry looked up from her thoughts. They were in the nurses' pretty green-and-peach dining room. The new probationers were giving the usual performance of new probationers. Cherry had to grin in spite of herself.

"Somebody ought to adopt them," she said casually. "One apiece."

The other girls pounced on her suggestion. "If someone had only adopted me in those first misguided weeks!" Marie Swift exclaimed. And Josie said, "You mean those first nerve-racking days, don't you?" Mai Lee declared that she had already singled out the little shy one for her adoptee.

"Now, now!" Cherry said hastily. "I don't mean we should turn ourselves into a day nursery this minute! Heavens, we're still awfully green ourselves. I mean when we're seniors, maybe." Self-doubt as to her own nursing ability assailed her: would she ever be a senior?

"All right! When we're seniors!" the girls chorused and at once fell to making plans. Almost two and a half years in advance.

Cherry smiled and went back to her brooding. If her fellow nurses guessed what a tremendous secret she was stuffed with, they would not be talking about probationers. All she could think of was the strange patient who had entered the erstwhile "Broom Closet" just a week ago tonight. Bits of the mystery were unraveling. Curiously, she had never seen the mysterious Miss Hall.

Vivian Warren flew over to their table, out of breath and glowing, and flung herself into a chair. Cherry dismissed the mystery for a moment.

"I've got it!" Vivian exclaimed. "Oh, I'm so happy! I've got my government scholarship! Now I can go on with my nursing training!" She turned involuntarily to Cherry.

"I'm so glad," Cherry said, and she meant it. The other girls pressed Vivian with their congratulations.

"And that's not all!" Vivian told them importantly. "Do you know that half of the probies coming in now are on government scholarships? Miss Reamer told me they're aided by the U. S. Cadet Nurse Corps."

Gwen gave a low whistle. "They sure must need nurses, to give training *and* maintenance free!"

"That's not exactly news," Marie Swift said. "Always need more nurses in wartime. Not only on the battle fronts either. Look at the shortage right here in Spencer, with nurses leaving for war fronts."

"No, no, not only because of the war!" Vivian said. "We'll be needed just as much after the war. Nursing isn't just a temporary war job. There is an awful shortage of nurses. It's a war job with a future."

They looked around at the new probationers. Most of them were the girls' own age, about eighteen, like Cherry and Ann and Gwen, but they saw a number of women in their twenties and thirties, too. Two new faces were frankly thirty-five. Some were only seventeen.

"And the older ones need adopting just as much as the infants," Ann said. "A probie is a desperate stricken creature, no matter what her age." And they gave themselves up to candidly enjoying seeing someone else struggle through the discomfiture they themselves had only barely graduated from.

"We're not adopting-seniors yet," Cherry reminded them as they all rose from the table. "Where are you bound for now?"

"The lake. Not just for the moonlight, either," Gwen said. "We want to look longingly at where we're going to throw our black stockings when we graduate."

"You have senioritis tonight," Cherry teased. "Take

a look for me. I'm going to squeeze in a nap before I go on night duty."

They said good night and Cherry went back alone to the Nurses' Residence.

In her own cozy little room, she shut the door, dimmed the lamp and lay down on the bed. It was quiet and balmy, but she did not sleep. She had too much thinking to do.

Step by step she went over the broken bits of information she possessed. By now she was sure that the patient brought in, in the dead of night, had not come from another wing of the hospital, but from the outside. The haste and secrecy pointed to that, as did the pile of airplane luggage. Certainly it had been a strange round-about way of bringing in a new admission.

He was a new admission, of that Cherry was certain. She got that far and then she was stumped. Why did she never see Miss Hall? Why did she never see Dr. Wylie enter, or food go in there?

There must be another entrance, probably on the fire stairs, Cherry figured. That explained Dr. Wylie and the matter of food. Of course the food might come up by dumb-waiter. As for Miss Hall, Cherry remembered having seen another room beyond the bathroom. Miss Hall was no doubt living there.

But there was something else. Every night since the mysterious patient had been shut up in there—and everyone still believed it was only a broom closet, as labeled—Cherry had heard voices. Masculine voices in that room, around midnight every night. Sometimes as many as a dozen. And once she had seen a man wandering around the corridor as if he were lost. She had known better than to approach him, and he had quickly disappeared. That meant that the patient, whoever he was, had secret night visitors.

And what did all this add up to? Cherry sighed. She could not guess, except that the ill man was important and was handling some affairs of the utmost secrecy. Since the other men came to him, he must be at the head of something. And that was as far as Cherry could get. She had plenty of ideas but no facts to check them with. She wished she could talk this over with Jim Clayton, or with sympathetic Marjory Baker. But Dr. Wylie had told her not to talk and never to go in there—on pain of expulsion. And that would be something Jim Clayton could not save her from.

Jim . . . She really ought to stop thinking about Jim Clayton. Mooning around when she ought to be studying. And Jim would not have any use for her if she were not a good nurse. Cherry still had plenty of doubts about herself. There was over two years to go— would she make it? Would her dream of nursing hold up under the strain of such things as Dr. Wylie and cranky patients and that tough surgical clinic? Jim had bucked her up over and over again. "If it hadn't been for him," Cherry thought gratefully, "I might have lost faith in myself. Wobbly as that faith is."

And maybe, Cherry thought, it was those buckings-up she felt so emotionally about, and not Jim himself. Maybe she was not in love with Jim at all. Maybe it was just gratitude and this delicious spring weather. "Marjory Baker could tell me," Cherry thought with a smile. Her first head nurse was by this time a real friend. "I'm lucky. Clayton and Baker—two of the nicest people in the hospital—for my friends."

Then she noticed with surprise that her battered alarm clock pointed to five minutes of eleven. She got up and sprinted across the lawn for the ward. Late, always late. Now she had missed her ten-thirty supper; how would she ever hold out until seven o'clock breakfast? Time always had been her worst enemy, she mourned as she raced into the shadowy ward, almost on time. The relief nurse, who was not too cooperative at any time, glowered at Cherry and left her alone with the patients on the silent darkened ward.

Cherry made the rounds with the flashlight, her rubber soles squishing on the linoleum floor. All quiet, everyone asleep for once. She returned to the desk, and in the lamp's circle of light, began filling out the night report, when an extraordinary flash came from the call board in the private pavilion across the hall. The call board really belonged to the private pavilion, but it was near enough for Cherry to see and hear it. This flash stuttered and broke.

Cherry knew what it was. She had seen it occasionally, briefly, two of the past seven nights. It was Room 3—the secret room. Dr. Wylie had omitted to have it disconnected. She tried not to pay any attention to the flash. She saw nurses passing in the private pavilion and they paid no attention to it.

But it flashed persistently tonight, so persistently that it worried her. Other nights it had flashed only briefly, as if someone in the room had brushed against it by accident. But Room 3 had been calling for five minutes now.

The supervisor came in. She was a tall, thin, dark woman, always reserved and cold and full of the importance of her position.

"Everything all right, Miss Ames? Are you watching Mr. Bond's temperature?" The supervisor lifted a cover, seemed satisfied. Cherry still saw the broken flash in the hall and wanted to say something to the supervisor. But she dared not give the secret away. She chose her words carefully.

"Is that call board broken by any chance?"

"Why?" The supervisor looked down the hall. "Oh, I see what you mean. That 3 is just an error. The electrician probably did not know that it only connects with the Broom Closet. Probably a crossed wire, that's all. Just ignore it, Miss Ames." She left.

But Cherry could not ignore it. Room 3 had been calling on and off for ten minutes now. That was no accidental brush, nor a crossed nor loose wire, either. That man was calling in there.

Something was wrong. Why should he be calling when his nurse was always with him? Or *was* Miss Hall with him? Cherry paced the ward uneasily, always returning to find that broken nervous flash before her eyes. She was getting jumpy herself. She went over to the door of the Broom Closet and, after looking around to see that no one was passing, rapped softly. There was no answer. She waited, rapped again. If Miss Hall were there, surely she would make a sign of some kind. There was no response. Miss Hall was not in there, Cherry guessed. That man was alone and signaling because he was in trouble.

Cherry's heart turned over. She was the only person around who knew the secret, and she was forbidden to go in there. She must locate Miss Hall at once. She ran to the elevator.

"I dunno her name, Miss, she's a strange nurse I never seen before," the elevator man told her. "She said, 'Take me down to the lab,' and I said, 'That's against the rules,' and she said, 'But I have Dr. Wylie's key,' and I said——"

Cherry thought rapidly, "If she had Dr. Wylie's key,

that's Miss Hall, all right. But what was she going to the lab for? Drug? Serum? If it was only for medicine, she could have gone to the apothecary. She needs a drug or a serum." She returned her attention to the elevator man.

"—so I waited like she said and she come back from the lab looking worried and not carrying nothing. About five minutes later, she rings again, and there she is in her hat and coat looking terribly worried and in an awful hurry. I take her down to the main lobby and she tells me again to keep mum and then goes out on the street. Almost running, she was." That meant, Cherry knew, Miss Hall had found no drug or serum in the laboratory which would be right or safe for the mysterious patient, and was going to another hospital or a commercial laboratory for it. At midnight!

Cherry frowned. "Did she say anything about Dr. Wylie?"

"She asked me where he was and if he came in to send him up to Miss Ames. Who's Miss Ames?" asked the elevator man.

"I'm—" Cherry started and then checked herself. So they were using her name as a signal! "Miss Ames is not important. And it really is a secret."

The man gaped. "Shouldn't I've told you?"

"I'm the one person it's all right to tell. But for goodness' sake, don't mention it to another soul."

"I won't, Miss. But I don't understand all this foolishness." The elevator man closed the car door, shaking his head, and Cherry heard the elevator slide down the shaft.

From then on Cherry moved fast. She phoned Dr. Wylie's office. He was not there. She phoned Dr. Wylie's home. He was not there, either. He had left with three men. No, they did not know where he was if not at the hospital. Cherry left a message that he call Miss Ames and hung up, thinking.

Room 3 had been flashing for fifteen minutes now. It was midnight and the relief nurse came in, so Cherry could take a brief rest period. She was afraid to leave. Cherry waved her aside. "But I may need you to take over the ward a little later," she said.

"Really, Ames, I don't understand you," the relief nurse said pettishly. "I'm not here just for your personal convenience." She marched off again.

"Oh, Lord, I've offended her!" Cherry thought. With all her other worry, she'd have to deal later with an uncooperative relief nurse. But there was no time to worry. What was the best way to deal with her responsibility and still not bare the secret? She should, Cherry knew, in ordinary circumstances, go to the supervisor and let the supervisor take over the responsibility. Very well, she'd try again with the supervisor. She'd drop a broader hint this time and see what she could learn. Almost running, she found the supervisor at her desk.

"Why aren't you on your ward? Have you left your

ward alone?" the supervisor demanded. "Certainly I'm sure. Of course there's no one in Room 3. There used to be a suite of rooms there, but the private pavilion never used it because it was expensive and inconvenient. About a year ago we closed it up. Nonsense, Miss Ames, you must be dreaming. I told you it was only a crossed wire, didn't I?"

Cherry made a guarded reply and sped back to her ward. She made a quick check-up, flashlight in hand, and found everything all right. The flash from Room 3 was coming weakly and irregularly now. But it was still coming. She must do something, and quickly! But what? Cherry racked her brain.

She had been forbidden to enter the room. Send a doctor in. That had to be done by supervisor's order and the supervisor simply did not believe Cherry. "All right," Cherry thought. "I'll get a doctor in there on my own. Someone I know and trust. Who's on night duty?" She thought hopefully of Dr. Freeman, then remembered that he had been transferred. Cherry did not know the present interne, Dr. Low. Dr. "Ding" Jackson would understand. She phoned Emergency Ward. This was his night off. Dr. Wylie probably had no assisting doctor on this case. She wondered if, by any miracle, Jim Clayton might be on night duty. She phoned the central operator and inquired. Jim was on tonight! That was a piece of luck.

"How can I come up there when you won't even

give me a reason?" his deep voice boomed over the wire.

"Oh, please, please!" Cherry begged into the phone. "I can't tell you—won't you take my word for it?"

She heard him laughing. "But it's against all the rules. Get your supervisor, Cherry. You mustn't take things into your own hands."

No, but she must not let that man in there die, either. Why would no one believe her? She hung up discouragedly. No patient must be left alone to die, and this man was an important man whose death might mean a great deal to many, many people. That much she could sense. She stood there trembling, trying to decide between the rules of medical ethics and the age-old dictum, "The patient must be saved at all costs!"

"A fine nurse I am!" she thought disgustedly. "Well, here's where I get myself expelled!"

Turning her back recklessly on her sleeping ward, she ran to the door of Room 3 and tried it. It was locked. She had expected that. Then she slipped noiselessly out to the fire stairs. In the dim light she found the door she had guessed must be there. The knob turned easily in her hand, and the door opened.

Cherry found herself in a conventional hospital room. Women's clothes were strewn around it. Miss Hall's room, she thought, and pushed hastily through the bathroom. In the room beyond, she stopped, staring.

In the half-light was the strangest hospital room she

had ever seen. The bed, table, chairs and bureau were conventional enough. But the windows had been veiled with an extra pair of thick draperies, tightly shut and stirring a little from the open window. On the walls were large maps, with thumbtacks of different colors stuck in them. They were not ordinary maps. There was a telephone, and Cherry saw it had an outside wire. What was going on in here? Cherry started as her eye fell on a curious small machine. She knew from Charlie's military manual what it was—a short-wave radio which received messages in code. A pair of earphones lay beside it, a crammed brief case, and beside that, a revolver.

Cherry started to back away in fear. This was a secret which was too dangerous to know.

Just then, the big figure in the bed moaned and cried out loudly, "Tell Kendall not to delay the action! Tell Kendall we can't hold here much longer! Tell Kendall —" He fell back, delirious.

Suddenly it was all clear to Cherry. The man was a soldier. An American—an ally? His voice had a curious intonation but it was so weak Cherry could not be sure of his nationality. An important commander, a man who led whole armies, from the looks of the room. Helpless, ill, and here he was all alone! Cherry sprang to the bed. Next to his side, a dressing was wet with blood. She took his temperature, pulse and respiration.

They were raging. She knew now what she must do. Rules or no rules. Let her get expelled. It was more important to save this military leader.

"I'll be right back," she whispered to the delirious man. "I'll bring help." She did not know whether he understood her or not. His face—he was about fifty—was strongly boned and the flesh drawn taut with illness. Under heavy sick lids, his eyes were like an eagle's. The broad, bony shoulders and the great frame seemed to dwarf the hospital bed. It was strange to see such a powerful man helpless. "I'll get help!" Cherry repeated, and this time he nodded a little.

Back out the way she came, Cherry ran to find the relief nurse. She was knitting peacefully in the nurses' sitting room.

"You've got to take my ward, you've got to, please!" Cherry begged.

"I suppose you're ready now!" the other girl sniffed. "But perhaps I'm not ready to relieve you."

"I'll pay you back with any favor you want!" Cherry pleaded. "Please——"

"Oh, all right," the other girl said grudgingly. She came back to the ward with Cherry. Cherry took a quick glance. Nothing untoward seemed to have happened in the few minutes she was away.

"Will you stay here until I get back?" Cherry asked gravely. "Believe me, it's a real emergency or I wouldn't bother you. You won't leave the ward alone, will you?"

"Well, I must say this is all awfully strange. I won't promise to stay. I'm not assigned here." Cherry left the other nurse, hoping she could get back soon, hoping the relief nurse would stay. Cherry could not be sure . . . And the ward *must* not be left alone, she thought, as she rang central operator again.

"Will you try Dr. Wylie's office once more?" Cherry could hear the operator ringing. No one replied. "Has anyone—a Miss Hall—left a message?" There was a moment's silence and then the operator said no. "Dr. Clayton, then, please." Cherry took a deep breath.

"Jim! You've got to come! It's a matter of life and death for more than just one man! It's the most important thing that ever happened to this hospital!"

"Why, Cherry, you sound almost hysterical. What is——"

"I'm not hysterical. It's the truth, I'm telling you! You've got to come!"

There was a moment's pause and then Dr. Clayton said doubtfully, "All right, I'll be right up."

"Hurry!" Cherry jiggled the hook. "Operator. Please ring Dr. Wylie's home again and tell him or leave word that Miss Ames needs him at once. Urgently. Yes, that's it. Thanks."

Well, now she'd done all she could to keep within the rules. If only Miss Hall would come back. But Miss Hall would have a long search, at this hour of the night, to find a hospital laboratory or a commercial laboratory open and one that had exactly the drug or serum she needed. Miss Hall probably was scouring the city. "She's a brave woman," Cherry thought.

And here was Jim Clayton, striding out of the self-service elevator into the shadowy corridor. Cherry had never been so glad to see anyone in her life. She rushed toward him, motioning him to be quiet.

"What is all this?" he demanded softly. But his face was serious and he followed Cherry obediently as she led him quickly out to the fire stairs. They entered the dim suite and Cherry led Dr. Clayton into the forbidden room.

His eyes widened as Cherry's had, as he saw the mute evidences of the maps, the code radio, the gun. He turned to her, questions in his face. She whispered quickly all the little information she had, and swore him to secrecy. "That's a very sick man," Jim Clayton muttered back, and went forward to the bed.

He examined the mysterious patient quickly and frowned. "The suture has broken. There's an internal hemorrhage. He needs an operation at once. If he does not bleed to death, the displacement of the adjoining organ may be fatal. I don't like this!" He looked up at Cherry, deeply troubled.

"What—what is it you don't like? she whispered back.

"The whole thing—I shouldn't know this secret—

I have no authority to operate—but most of all, I don't like this man's condition! And as if that weren't enough —" For a moment he covered his face with his hand.

"What is it?" Cherry whispered tensely.

"To operate—immediately—we'd need a local anaesthetic. This is one of those rare and special cases where we can't use novocaine, or anything similar. Have to use something else—though I don't know what would do the trick, unless it is one of those new Russian anaesthetics. I understand Dr. Ketchum over at City Hospital has got some of them. By George! That's obviously where his nurse has gone! She's gone to Ketchum. Without the right thing, we can't operate. And if we delay operating——"

"Give him ether?" Cherry whispered. "Spinal anaesthetic?"

Jim Clayton shook his head. "No, this is a special kind of case."

The curtains stirred, like a sigh. The man on the bed moaned deliriously. Cherry turned cold. There was so much at stake in this secret room. Victory itself, perhaps.

"What a responsibility!" Jim Clayton said desperately.

Cherry whirled to him and gripped his arm. Her fingers bit into his flesh like steel in her excitement. "We have a drug! We have it! Why didn't I think of it before!" She reminded him about Dr. Joe's drug, lying unused down there in the laboratory. Unused, she thought ironically, when it was needed most!

"But it hasn't been accepted," Dr. Clayton whispered back worriedly.

"It's been tested—it works—" She waited, looking at him.

"It's this man's only chance," the young doctor admitted slowly.

Just then they heard the fire stairs door open. Footsteps groped through the darkened rooms. Then they saw Dr. Wylie standing authoritatively in the doorway. Cherry was so relieved to see the surgeon that she forgot to be afraid.

"How is he?" Dr. Wylie demanded, and strode directly to the bed. "Miss Ames! What's happened? Where's Miss Hall?"

Cherry told him what she knew. Dr. Wylie sized up the man's critical condition in a glance. Cherry knew what he was thinking. She ventured to tell him about Dr. Joe's drug, downstairs for the taking.

Dr. Wylie bit his lip. "That drug has been tested on three volunteers and I know it works. But it has not yet been officially accepted, so technically that drug's an unknown quantity. If I were to use it, unsanctioned as it is, I would be committing a breach of medical ethics. And there is one chance in a hundred that it would mean taking a chance with his life."

"It works, I know it works!" Cherry pleaded. "It's been tested most carefully! The Board surely must approve it when they meet in July! I know the man who discovered and developed it! Oh, Dr. Wylie, don't you remember the successful demonstration—" Cherry put into her voice all her belief in Dr. Joe.

Dr. Wylie glanced at young Dr. Clayton, and looked back at the patient. He shut his eyes tightly for a moment, then said, "You're right, Miss Ames. It's questionable procedure but we'll have to do it. Miss Ames, go get that drug. We can't move him. Bring me O.R. equipment. Be sure your hands are clean." He handed her the keys. "Clayton, you'll have to assist me. I don't want anyone else to know and as long as you know already—" His voice faded as Cherry dashed out.

She shook all the time her flashlight picked out the precious vial in the darkened laboratory. She shook as she raced into the operating room, spread a sterile sheet on a wheeled table, with a sterile forceps picked up and flung on it everything she thought Dr. Wylie would need, covered the O.R. equipment with another sterile sheet and raced upstairs with it. She had never even seen an operation and here she was about to assist at one! Well, Dr. Wylie would tell her what she must do. She prayed that in her ignorance, she would not make some fatal mistake.

What happened next was like a nightmare. Everything went so fast, everything was so difficult and strange to Cherry. She felt as if she were running at top speed through a trance of scrubbing the bathroom, scrubbing herself for an endless twenty minutes, setting up an emergency table. "Sterile! Sterile!" she kept muttering to herself dully. She saw—or did she dream it?—the surgeon preparing the patient, giving him a blood transfusion. The next thing she knew someone had turned on a cloaked but powerful lamp. Within that narrow blaze of light, Cherry briefly moved, re-making the bed with sterile sheets, helping the two men into sterile gowns, gloves, masks.

Suddenly, just as he was about to start, Dr. Wylie lifted his eyes to their faces. "Do you know who this man is?" he said sternly. "He is General—" And he spoke a name which Cherry and Jim heard with the profoundest respect, one of the greatest names of their time. He had been wounded and had been flown to the United States.

Half-hypnotized by Dr. Wylie's tense whispered orders, Cherry acted as anaesthetist. Jim Clayton was hovering somewhere beside him. Out of hurry and urgency and the blinding circle of light, one thing stood out firm and solid for Cherry. She saw Dr. Wylie administer Dr. Joe's drug! At last it was being used, and by a great surgeon! Would it hold? Would it work? Tookie the cat, drugged, floated before her eyes. The patient stirred and spoke. Dr. Wylie's voice came and went out of the shadow behind the brilliant lamp. Time melted.

"Eighty-four, pulse weak," she heard her own voice say.

"All right, Clayton. Incision."

Jim's gloved hands came within Cherry's range of vision, moved, withdrew.

"Scalpel, Miss Ames."

The patient murmured something. The surgeon's hands, light and quick as butterflies, lifted tiny delicate living parts.

"Clamp."

Jim Clayton moved forward, receded again into the dense gloom. They worked in breathless silence. For how long, Cherry did not know. The surgeon's terse commands, a pause, a reassuring word to the patient, a rustle—that was all. Cherry did not understand all she saw, knew she would not understand until as a senior she would work in the O.R.'s

Finally Dr. Wylie stepped back with a heavy sigh. His eyes above the gauze mask drooped with exhaustion.

"All right, Clayton. Finish up." The young doctor carefully closed the incision and bandaged it.

It was all over. The patient was all right. The drug had held.

They went into the next room, leaving the patient to rest. They were just stripping off their gloves and masks when a strange woman burst in, and behind her, the three mysterious men Cherry had seen that first night.

"You're here, sir!" the woman said in relief. She was a tall middle-aged woman, stern-faced, and under her coat Cherry saw a nurse's white dress. Miss Hall. She fumbled in her bag, distressed, and held out a vial to Dr. Wylie. "I knew you'd need this—it may not be right but it's the best thing there is. I tried all over the city to find Dr. Ketchum and couldn't. Then my taxi stalled on the express highway and I was frantic." She looked anxiously at the surgeon. "Forgive me for leaving the patient, sir. I shouldn't have—but I couldn't reach you—I couldn't reach anyone—I couldn't tell anyone! I couldn't stand by and let him die! There was nothing else I could do!" The three men behind her were anxious beyond speech.

Dr. Wylie nodded. "You did the right thing, Miss Hall. I got your message—also Miss Ames's. We won't need this now," he indicated the vial. "I've operated. He's all right."

A sigh went up from all the newcomers.

Then the man in the unknown uniform said sharply, "Who are these two? What right have they in here?"

Through the open door came the General's voice, very weak. "The little girl—she saved my life."

Everyone looked at Cherry and she had an idiotic impulse to say, "Who, me?" Yes, he really did mean her. Cherry Ames. She was frightened, a little, under all those examining eyes, and stepped closer to Jim Clayton. He took her hand comfortingly. They smiled at each other. They had been through a good deal together this night.

"This student nurse had no right to come in here," Dr. Wylie said. Cherry, tired as she was, felt a wave of fury. She turned on Dr. Wylie and for the first time in the long history of her feud with the surgeon, she fought back.

"If I hadn't broken your orders, the General would be dead by now!" she cried at him. "And you can't blame Dr. Clayton, either!"

Dr. Wylie shut his mouth tightly and looked down at the floor. Two of the men whispered. Then to Cherry's surprise, Dr. Wylie said in a chastened voice, "You're quite right, Miss Ames. You did save his life." He added stiffly, "I beg your pardon." He turned his back. "You two may go now."

But barring the door was the man in uniform. He looked at them gravely. "Under no circumstances are you to tell anyone the General is here!" Then he looked deep into their eyes and said with the greatest emphasis, "Should his army know he is temporarily not in command, it would do their courage no good. Should the enemy know this, it would be the signal for an attack." He paused. "Now do you understand?"

Shaken, Cherry and Jim Clayton said, "Yes." Then

they were permitted to leave. The door closed, the lock clicked, and they knew they would never enter that forbidden room again.

They stood for a moment in the fire hall, utterly exhausted. "It's half past three," Jim Clayton said irrelevantly.

Only then did Cherry remember. "My ward!" Had the reluctant relief nurse stayed? What had been happening on the ward? She pushed open the heavy door frantically, and ran out.

There in the hall was the floor supervisor, very angry. She was waiting for her and pounced on Cherry as she came through the door.

"The relief nurse reported you," the floor supervisor whispered sharply. Reported her! What a rotten thing to do! "Why did you go off and leave your ward? What sort of nurse are you?"

"But I left a nurse in charge—I—" Cherry leaned tiredly against the wall. She wondered herself what sort of nurse she was. Jim Clayton stood near by, uncertain, unable to help her.

Cherry looked at the supervisor. "A great deal went wrong," she said earnestly. She was heartsick that she could not explain. "I can't tell you about it but Dr. Wylie can."

"Dr. Wylie," the floor supervisor exclaimed unbelievingly. She looked Cherry up and down.

"Return to your ward, Miss Ames. Dr. Wylie indeed! I only hope he backs you up!"

Aching with fatigue and nervous let-down, too tired even to worry any more, Cherry went back into the sleeping ward. It seemed a year since she had been in here. She dragged herself from bed to bed with her flashlight. Everyone was sleeping quietly. She wondered numbly how she could stay awake until seven in the morning.

A rustle at the door caught her attention. She was shocked at what she saw. Apparently this night's excitement was not over yet! And yet in a way, she had to smile, they looked so right together. Jim Clayton and Marjory Baker were clasped in each other's arms.

They came toward Cherry, half-guilty and smiling. "Well, now you know our secret," Marjory Baker whispered, "and I'm glad you're the first to know, because you're——"

"Some hour for romance, huh?" Jim said. "Would you have thought——"

"I was on duty tonight and phoned Jim and he was off his ward for two hours—well, I was worried, so I came up here," Marjory Baker explained.

"Cherry, do you give us your blessing?" Jim laughed. And Cherry most emphatically did.

They both talked at once. They looked so happy, they were so obviously and deeply in love, that Cherry wondered how she could have missed seeing the truth. It was a happy truth, too. "They're perfect together," Cherry thought as she watched them disappear into the shadows of the corridor. There went her romance. But it was all right, Cherry thought happily. Her two favorite people in the hospital—it was perfect. Reeling as she was with fatigue, Cherry realized she was not really in love with Jim—or with anybody. She was in love with nursing.

"And maybe it's going to be an unrequited love," she thought wearily as she wrote in the order book and wondered what Dr. Wylie would say for her tomorrow. Right now, she was just too tired to worry. She had done her best—and if it had been wrong, then she just was not meant to be a nurse. The gnawing self-doubts crept back but she pushed them away. That would be decided for her, tomorrow. She was too tired to think any more.

It was only at seven that morning, when Cherry walked slowly across the lawn under a clear blue sky and listened to the birds singing, that she realized something. One big thing emerged strongly and wonderfully out of the night's tangled experience. Until now, Dr. Joe's drug had been used only on the three test cases. Now it had been used in actual practice— and by an authoritative surgeon—and it had worked! It was that much nearer official acceptance now! His worries were almost over! The load on Cherry's heart lifted and she relaxed.

"Why, it's a miracle," she whispered to herself. "Without meaning to, I've almost solved Dr. Joe's problem! Surely Dr. Wylie will endorse the drug now! Think of the people that drug's going to save!" She looked up at the coral streaks in the early morning sky as if she had never seen the sun before. "Why, that's what matters! Even if I never can be a nurse, Dr. Joe's drug is closer to being accepted! Even if *I* fail, I've accomplished that!"

She walked on alone across the lawn with a new courage coming to life within her.

CHAPTER XII

Farewell and Hail!

THERE WAS A NOTE UNDER CHERRY'S DOOR WHEN SHE woke up. It read:

Report to Training School Office at 3 P.M.
                              M. R. Reamer

It was strange to have to hide the note, and to be unable to tell Ann and Gwen about the interview she faced. At three o'clock, Cherry reluctantly went into Miss Reamer's office, all alone.

Dr. Wylie and the Superintendent of Nurses were seated across from her on the other side of Miss Reamer's desk.

"Sit down, Miss Ames," Miss Reamer said, pleasantly enough.

Cherry gratefully dropped into a chair, smoothing her blue and white striped uniform. She did not know how much longer, after this talk, she would be allowed to wear that beloved uniform and cap.

Dr. Wylie cleared his throat. He looked at her uncompromisingly as ever. "My colleague and I have been discussing what happened last night. Miss Reamer, as you may or may not have guessed, and as not even Miss Hall knows, has been aware of the—er—unusual situation from the beginning." Cherry had not known that. That helped matters. Or did it? "What Miss Reamer did not know was that you were involved in—er—it."

Miss Reamer looked at Cherry with an amused smile. "You certainly were involved last night, weren't you, Miss Ames?" Cherry breathed easier.

"I only did what I thought was right," she said.

"Hmm. You told me as much last night," Dr. Wylie said dryly, "in no uncertain terms." He glared at Cherry. "You're a spunky young woman, even if you are impertinent. And I must ask you again to take off that rouge!" Cherry sighed and glanced at Miss Reamer, who bit her twitching lips and hastily looked at the floor. "To get back to the point, I feel that you are to be congratulated on your courage and initiative. You are really a nurse."

Cherry gripped the arms of her chair, not sure she was hearing correctly. Really a nurse, he said!

Both Dr. Wylie and Miss Reamer were smiling at her now. "Then I'm not to be— But I left my ward and the relief nurse reported me!"

Miss Reamer leaned forward. "Don't worry, my dear.

This will not be a demerit on your record—quite the contrary."

Cherry looked at them both and blinked. "Then—then it's all right?" she managed to get out.

"It's more than all right. I said I congratulated you, didn't I?" Dr. Wylie said as gruffly as ever. He stood up. "I understand you know Dr. Joseph Fortune, the discoverer of the anaesthetic we used last night?"

Cherry smiled. "I've known him since my first breath, sir."

"Do you suppose he would be interested in coming to the hospital to discuss doing further research in our laboratories? His drug needs a little more testing on volunteer patients, and it needs a minor improvement or two, to make it entirely perfect and acceptable."

"Would he!" Cherry sprang to her feet. "Oh, Dr. Wylie, it's what he's always dreamed of! And what I've always hoped for him!"

"Hmm. Fine. Very good." Cherry saw how embarrassed Dr. Wylie was at her happiness. She caught Miss Reamer's twinkle of amusement. "Give me his address and I'll invite him to come to talk with me at once." He stalked out.

Cherry and Miss Reamer sat there looking at each other, all but laughing. "He's an old darling and an old bluff," Cherry thought. Well, her feud with Dr. Wylie was finally over. She saw that Miss Reamer was studying her.

"You're very tired, aren't you, Miss Ames? I think you've happened to draw the heaviest assignments of any first-year student, this year, and then last night . . . I recommend that you take your month's vacation earlier than usual. I'll arrange it so that you do not miss any of your work when you return."

"But I was looking forward to Children's Ward," Cherry cried, "and all the other girls will be going on——"

"The hospital and your classmates all will be here when you get back," Miss Reamer assured her. "I think a month of breakfasts in bed and forgetting all about nursing is what you need just now."

"I'll never forget about nursing," Cherry said as Miss Reamer took her to the door.

"I know you won't. You are a fine student, Miss Ames, and you are going to make a fine nurse."

Cherry went out into the lobby rather dazed. All those doubts about whether she would make a nurse gone, now! Gone and on the best authority! Cherry almost danced through the corridors.

She was so happy and she longed to share her happiness and excitement with Ann and Gwen. But she dare not say a word to anyone, for that might lead to questions on the secret of the forbidden room. And just because she dare not talk and was bursting to, she had to meet all the people she would have loved to have told! Ruth Schwartz and Miss Mac stopped her in the hall, and at the door to the yard Dr. Freeman and Dr. "Ding" Jackson called after her. Mai Lee and Bertha and Josie and Ann and Gwen called to her from the lounge. If she got to talking to *them,* she would burst! Cherry fled. She sought out Dr. Jim Clayton in the small, deserted reference library.

"Hello!" he said. He looked very sleepy. "I certainly am glad to see you. I'm going to explode if I don't talk to someone. Can't even tell Marjory. Do you feel the same way?"

Cherry nodded and perched on his desk. He put down the pamphlet he was studying and tilted his feet up. They beamed at each other. It was nice to know that, Marjory Baker or no Marjory Baker, they were still the best of friends. "Just like it always was," Cherry thought with satisfaction. "I guess that proves I wasn't in love with him. And I'm so fond of Marjory that it couldn't be nicer."

"What a night!" Jim Clayton said. "Are you all straightened out with the powers that be?"

Cherry nodded and told him, too, of Dr. Wylie's forthcoming invitation to Dr. Joe. Jim Clayton was glad, she could see it.

Marjory Baker came in just then. She, too, looked very sleepy, her clear hazel eyes heavy and her soft blonde hair flying about a wan little face. "What a night!" she greeted them. "Jim says I mustn't ask about last night's mysterious comings and goings, but it looks as if you two were conspirators! And what are you two up to now?" She sat down beside Cherry, her feet dangling. "Doctor, what do you think of my little probie being entrusted with night duty already?" She looked at Cherry proudly.

"I think your little ex-probie looks tired," Jim said.

And Cherry really was very tired. Now that the tension was over, and she began to relax, she realized Miss Reamer was right.

She was transferred to Men's Medical and did her routine work there rather automatically. What really kept her interested was the prospect of Dr. Joe's visit to the hospital. It would be wonderful to see him successful, after that lonely struggle. And it would be interesting to see Dr. Joe and Dr. Wylie together. Cherry was a bit doubtful as to how the two men would get along. A mere student nurse would not be invited to the interview, anyway. Dr. Joe would tell her all about it afterwards. And Dr. Joe would tell her too, she hoped, all the news of Hilton and her family and Midge.

Cherry was walking past the private pavilion one afternoon with Ann and Gwen when they passed the door marked "Broom Closet." They had just come off duty and stood there waiting for the elevator.

"Funny place for a broom closet," Ann remarked observantly.

"Yes, isn't it," Gwen said. Her lively freckled face was all curiosity.

Cherry held her breath. "I don't think so," she said loudly.

Just then one of the maids, whom Cherry had known on Men's Orthopedic, came by with a bucket and a mop.

"Hello, Miss Ames," the maid said, importantly jangling the bunch of keys at her belt. "It's kind of tame around here without you. Plenty of excitement when you were around."

"Uh—is that so?" Cherry said. Did the maid know anything? She could not take her eyes off the little figure in the black dress and white apron, for the maid was fitting a key into the "Broom Closet" door. The door swung open. The room was full of pails, brooms, ironing boards. The bed, the maps, the mystery general were gone. Cherry blinked. Maybe she had dreamed the whole thing.

"There, you see," Gwen was saying, "it *is* a closet, Ann." And the three of them stepped into the elevator. "What are you muttering, Cherry? It sounds to me like 'broom closet, broom closet, broom closet.'"

"It is," Cherry said. "Never mind, children. Ames is a sad case but not violent. Would you hate me if I had a secret I didn't tell you?" she said suddenly.

"No!" they chorused.

Ann added, "We guarantee to love you under any and all circumstances. Not that we wouldn't adore knowing a secret, but we are too polite to inquire."

And Gwen said with a grin, "A secret is something

you *don't* tell. I'm a good deal more interested in getting a chocolate soda."

So they went off and had a chocolate soda apiece, happily ruining their appetites for dinner. "They're good, understanding, unselfish friends," Cherry thought gratefully. It was going to be fun going through junior and senior years with them.

Cherry was busy on Men's Medical Ward one hot afternoon when the ward phone rang and she was told to report to T.S.O. That did not alarm her as it once might have. She pinned her cap more firmly in place, wished for a clean apron, and ran down to Miss Reamer's office. But Miss Reamer was not there. Instead, she found Dr. Wylie and Dr. Joe.

"Cherry!" He stood up and held out both hands to her. "How are you, child?" She ran to him, smiling at his untidy suit and his boyish shock of gray hair.

"Oh, Dr. Joe, has Dr. Wylie told you the wonderful news?"

Dr. Wylie looked a little startled at this warm reunion but he smiled. It was rather like an iceberg cracking, but Cherry was no longer afraid of the surgeon.

"Dr. Wylie has told me," Dr. Joe said in his deep slow voice, "what you did. Good girl! Midge is beside herself, about the way you've brought my drug to Dr. Wylie's attention. And so am I," he admitted with candor. The two men talked about the drug while Cherry watched them.

Cherry noticed that when Dr. Wylie looked at Dr. Joe, his grim face softened and he chuckled indulgently at some of Dr. Joe's artless, whole-hearted mannerisms. Dr. Joe, in his turn, treated the great surgeon with the same simple unimpressed friendliness he treated everyone, from Hilton's mayor to the ten-year-old delivery boy. But of the two, plain little Dr. Joe had the greater dignity and it was Dr. Wylie whose manner was respectful. Cherry was touched. If Dr. Wylie so frankly took his hat off to Dr. Joe, he was pretty nice at that.

"So you will come to the hospital and work in our laboratories?" Dr. Wylie said with undisguised eagerness. He made it sound as if it were Dr. Joe conferring the favor.

Dr. Joe's eyes shone. "I— Thank you, sir. Nothing would make me happier. I am exceedingly grateful to you for the opportunity."

"I believe deeply in your discovery. It saved a great man. Your drug, and Miss Ames alertness," Dr. Wylie said. Cherry had never heard Dr. Wylie talk like this before, never seen his old hawk face so relaxed. He was different in Dr. Joe's presence. "Will you come this fall?" he pressed Dr. Joe.

Dr. Joe smiled. "I would like to start in this very minute! You can be sure I'll come! But Hilton has a new clinic and they have asked me to contribute my services. And even more pressing, I am working on a derivative of this same drug and I ought to finish that part of the research first. I should like to think over a bit how I am going to arrange the research and divide my time between research and the clinic. Perhaps I shall have to divide the research between next year and the following year."

Cherry thought delightedly, "Then Dr. Joe will be here in either my junior or my senior years, or maybe both!"

The two men were shaking hands. "And to think I brought them together!" Cherry told herself in amazement.

"I hope you will be at the hospital when I am able to be here too," Dr. Wylie said. "I have been accepted for medical service with the Army, and where my work will take me, or when, is hard to know." Cherry remembered the rumor Bertha Larsen had hoped would come true for her. "Your drug should be extremely useful in work with soldiers." He held Dr. Joe's hand a moment longer. "Dr. Fortune, you remind me of my first teacher. A man who showed me the idealism of medicine."

So that explained Dr. Wylie's altered manner! Dr. Wylie revered Dr. Joe for the same reasons that Cherry loved him. She felt closer now to the terrible surgeon than she would have dreamed possible that first night he told her to "take off that rouge!"

On their way out, they met Miss Reamer. Apparently she had been introduced to Dr. Joe, for she greeted him, and said to Cherry, "You remember I told you you were to have your vacation soon, Miss Ames. How would you like to go back to Hilton with Dr. Fortune? It's all arranged."

"It will be a triumphal entry into the city for both of us," Dr. Joe smiled at Cherry as Miss Reamer disappeared into her office. They wandered across the lobby and out onto the lawn. "Cherry, do you remember the day you started off for nursing school?" Cherry nodded. It seemed long, long ago. "Do you remember you came to say good-by to me and you said you'd like to help me get my drug accepted and used? Well, Cherry, you've helped me beyond my wildest hopes! I want you to know how grateful I am." His gentle tired face in the May sunshine was radiant.

"Why—why, Dr. Joe," Cherry stammered. "Don't you ever dare to say thank you to *me*. You knew me way back when. Besides, it's you who steered me into nursing school in the first place. I ought to say thank you to you!"

"You like it?"

"Oh, yes, yes!"

"Those two people in the office told me you're going to be a fine nurse, Cherry. Tell me something. Do you feel like a nurse—that is, are you sure?"

"Yes, Dr. Joe," Cherry said softly. "For a while I didn't—I was unsure—afraid. But now I know."

It seemed to Cherry that the whole class came down

to the train. "Perhaps because it's Sunday afternoon and a beautiful summer's day and they're free anyway," she thought modestly. She hung out the train window trying to talk to everybody at once. Dr. Joe smiled from the opposite seat.

"Don't you dare work in the Children's Ward till I get back!" she half-enviously warned Ann and Gwen.

"Not even when Winky comes back?" Ann teased. "Oh, look, girls, she's wearing the gloves I gave her for her birthday!"

"How about my rubbers?" Gwen demanded. "And my garters!" Josie called. "Never mind them," Bertha Larsen said, slightly shocked, along with demure Mai Lee, at the mention of garters in public. "When you come back, I'll bake you another cake!"

Cherry glowed at them. "I can't wait to get back. In fact, I don't want to go at all!" It would be wonderful to see Mother and Dad and Charlie and Midge and Hilton itself and her gay little room. But the great white hospital was very dear to her now.

Vivian Warren did not say much. She just held on tightly to Cherry's hand and said, "Come back."

Dr. Jim Clayton and Marjory Baker, too, had come down to see Cherry off. They looked so handsome and so happy together, the tall, gay, dark young doctor and the very feminine blonde little nurse, that Cherry wished she had a picture of them to keep for always. Jim Clayton said:

"I have regards for you from—" he cleared his throat, took a deep breath and reeled off, "Peg McIntyre, Ruthie Schwartz, "Ding" Jackson, Hal Freeman, Mrs. "Cooky" Gaynor, the little Puerto Rican lady who's still lying on Orthopedic, the maid on Men's Orthopedic, believe it or not Miss Craig, Mr. O'Sullivan from the clinic and—Whew! Have I forgotten anybody?"

They all laughed and Cherry gripped her hands tight together. What a lot of friends she had made in this wonderful year!

The train was starting to move now and Dr. Joe put a warning hand on her arm. But Cherry still hung out the window, as they all called out to her, "Have fun!" "Think of us slaving while you're loafing!" "You're wanted on Hilton Ward, Miss Ames!" "Come back, Cherry!" "Come back!" "Come back!"

Yes, she would always go back—to the vast busy fortress of a hospital, to her friends, to her patients who needed her, to the nursing work that was the most exciting and important thing in her life. Cherry thought back fleetingly over the last year. Any last lingering doubts had been erased now, she had proven herself worthy, and she felt joyous and confident. Cherry knew, finally, that she was truly a nurse.

The laughter of her classmates echoed in her ears. The train roared toward Hilton, toward home. But her heart was in her other home, in the antiseptic-smelling corridors, in the peaceful wards with their white beds, in the cool gray stone-and-steel laboratory, in the bustling clinic and the gay crowded nurses' dining room and in the hot sweet air of the operating rooms. She could not wait to see what her next years of nurse's training would bring.